a pocketful of RHYME
Imagination for a new generation

2006 Poetry Competition for 7-11 year-olds

Young Writers

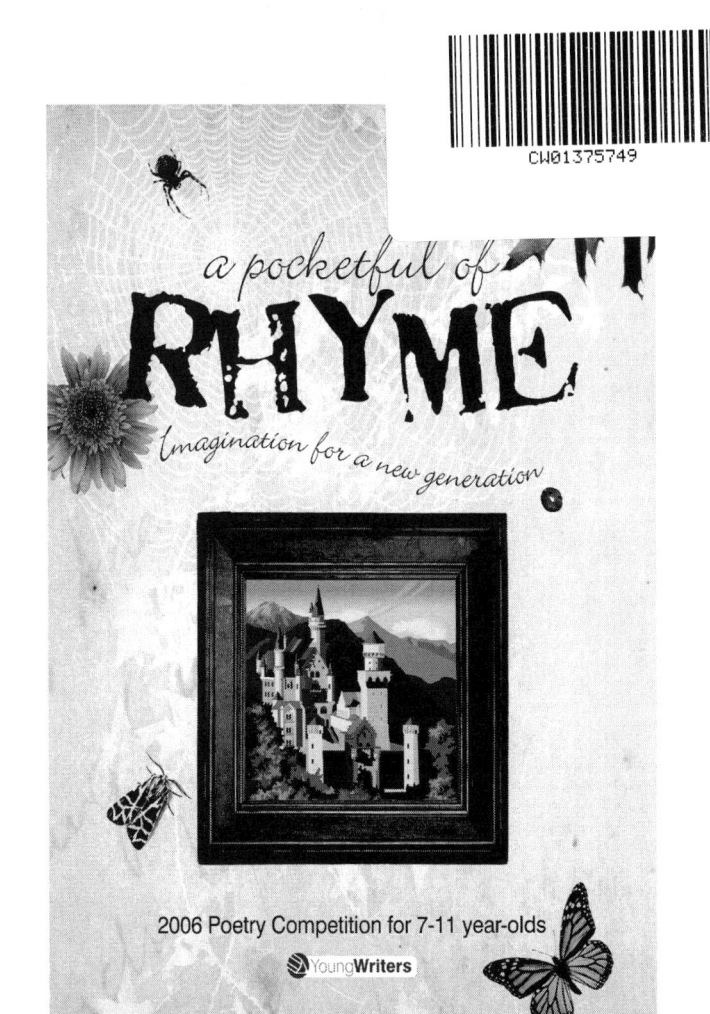

Welsh Voices
Edited by Annabel Cook

Young Writers

First published in Great Britain in 2007 by:
Young Writers
Remus House
Coltsfoot Drive
Peterborough
PE2 9JX
Telephone: 01733 890066
Website: www.youngwriters.co.uk

All Rights Reserved

© Copyright Contributors 2007

SB ISBN 978-1 84602 774 1

Foreword

Young Writers was established in 1991 and has been passionately devoted to the promotion of reading and writing in children and young adults ever since. The quest continues today. Young Writers remains as committed to the nurturing of poetic and literary talent as ever.

This year's Young Writers competition has proven as vibrant and dynamic as ever and we are delighted to present a showcase of the best poetry from across the UK and in some cases overseas. Each poem has been selected from a wealth of *A Pocketful Of Rhyme* entries before ultimately being published in this, our fourteenth primary school poetry series.

Once again, we have been supremely impressed by the overall quality of the entries we have received. The imagination, energy and creativity which has gone into each young writer's entry made choosing the poems a challenging and often difficult but ultimately hugely rewarding task - the general high standard of the work submitted ensured this opportunity to bring their poetry to a larger appreciative audience.

We sincerely hope you are pleased with this final collection and that you will enjoy *A Pocketful Of Rhyme Welsh Voices* for many years to come.

Contents

Aberaeron Primary School, Aberaeron
    Class Poem (Years 3 & 4)   1
    Megan Hawkins (7), Nadine Owens & Tristan Williams (8),
        Ifan & Megan Davies (9)   2
    Emily Harwood, Bethany Hughes, Thomas & Liam   3
    Bleddyn Thomas, Erin McCudden & Beth Davies & Ryan   4
    Sara Williams (7), Hannah, Tia Norris (9) & Jordan   5

Croesty Primary School, Pencoed
    Carys Rees (9)   6
    Ella Griffiths (8)   7
    William Morgan (10)   8
    Amy Field (9)   9
    Megan Bosley (8)   10
    Rhys Young   11
    Lewis Smith (9)   12
    Daniel Watkins (9)   12
    Daniel Weeks (8)   13
    Emily Ames (9)   14
    Josie Reffell (8)   15
    Owain Hicks (8)   16
    Ayesha Williams (9)   17
    Tom Stride (9)   18
    Ellie Woolhouse-Jones   19
    Justine Stark (9)   19
    Megan Griffiths   20
    Jamie Dyer   20
    Donovan Massebo (8)   21
    Katy Abbott   22
    Sam Rowland-Jones (8)   23
    Joshua Brown (8)   24
    Chris Cooper (9)   25
    Leah Eyre (9)   26
    Saffron Foster (9)   26
    Cerys Bethan Dyke (9)   27
    Alex Wilson (9)   27
    Jamie Powell (8)   28
    Ellyn Williams (9)   29
    Zoe Morgan (10)   30

Sarah Davies (9)	30
Megan Owen (9)	31
Joshua Maunder (9)	31
Taylor Johnson (9)	32
Harry Lock (9)	32
Elinor Taylor (9)	33
Olivia Bruford (9)	33
Lauren Sproul (10)	34
Corey Jeffrey Jones (10)	34
Benjamin Davies (9)	35
Nia Weston (9)	35
Nicole Sproul (10)	36
Emily Sims (9)	36
Matthew Cowell (8)	37
Elliot Clegg (9)	37
James Cattermole (9)	38
Thomas Pound (9)	38
Samuel Mark Bontempo (10)	39
Ellis Griffiths (9)	39
Emily Smith (8)	40
Ryan Frewen (9)	40
Jacob Hughes	41
Alex King (9)	41
Abbey Griffiths (8)	42
Callum Sparks (9)	42
Dylan Barrett (8)	43
Rosie Thomas (9)	43
Joe Thomas (8)	44
Liam Bowen (9)	44
Rhyse Edwards (8)	45
Chloe Chilcott (9)	46
Ben Gwyther (8)	47
Emily Coles (7)	48
Charlotte Morgan (8)	49
Scott Brown (8)	50
Rhys Butler (8)	51
Kieran Parrish	52
Joshua	53
Natalie Richards (7)	54
Dylan Grey	55
Cameron Fyvie-Davies (8)	56
Shereen Miers (8)	57

Zoe Jones (8)	58
Geddy Nash	59
Liam Hiett (7)	60
Dylan Davies	60

Llangeitho Primary School, Tregaron

Beatrice Angharad Wynne Edwards (11)	61
Catrin Pink (11)	62
Caitlin Culyer (9)	63
Jordan Gregory (9)	64

St Robert's Catholic Primary School, Aberkenfig

Megan Richards (8)	65
Liam Evans (11)	65
Ffion Randall (8)	66
Gina Bertorelli (8)	66
James Jones (8)	67
Holly Jade Bowen (10)	67
Emma Chumley (8)	68
Oliver Marks (8)	68
Aaron Hatch (9)	69
Ryan Nolan (9)	69
Amy Keepings (9)	70
Cristina Ferreira (8)	70
Charlotte Leston (9)	71
Holly Richards (9)	71
Constance Osgood-Finney (9)	72
Jonathan Russell (10)	72
Leah Roberts (9)	73
Jade Radcliffe (9)	73
Ffiôn Morgan (10)	74
Kristie Hore (9)	74
Jordan Young, Cameron Martin & Shane Lewis (9)	75
Sirage Bellia (10)	75
Lowrie Dean (9)	76
James Pare (9)	76
Bronte Marlborough (9)	77
Paige Coward (9)	77
Bethan John (9)	78
Catalin Mellor (9)	78
Isobel Rees (9)	79

Cian Watkins (9)	79
Matthew Roche (10)	80
Justyna Mikusek (10)	80
Natasha Evans (9)	81
Brógan Watkins (11)	81
Callum Smeaton (11)	82
Sorcha Davies (10)	82
Emily Thomas (11)	82
Shannon Bargery (11)	83
Joseph Hapgood (9)	83
Lydia Price (10)	84
Emma Dodd (10)	84
Jessica Buller (10)	85
Emilie James (10)	85
Taija Pengilly (11)	86
Laura Shillibier (10)	86
Jack Evans (10)	86
Jordan Hatch (11)	87
Peter Devonshire (11)	87
Ethan Marlborough (10)	87
Michael Thomas (10)	88
Sean Cooke (10)	88
Joshua Sage (11)	89
Joshua Paget-Howe (10)	89

Swiss Valley Primary School, Llanelli

Rosie Plimmer (9)	90
Ryan Samuel Davies (9)	90
Rhydian Glyn Ken Jones (9)	91
Amy Elise May Williams (9)	91
Lucy Cara Havard (9)	92
Kamran Raza (9)	93
Lyndsey Morris (9)	94
Conor Polson (9)	94
Amelia Thomas (9)	95
Bethan Harriet Jones (9)	95
Caitlin Lauren Evans (9)	96
Zoe Alexandra Austin (9)	96
Shauna Davies (9)	97
Rehaan Ahktaar (9)	97
Michael Robert Fry (9)	98

Kirsty Leigh Thomas (9)   99
Bethany Davies (9)   100

Talgarth Primary School, Brecon
Chirelle Morris (8)   100
Ben Peters (7)   101
Brynley Eckley (8)   101
Millie Jones (8)   102
Cellan Davies & Charmaine Carey (7)   102
Ceri Jones (7)   103
Ethan Hatton (7)   103
Jack Carey & Morgan Skyrme (8)   104
Corey Thompson (8)   104
Caitlin Pugh & Megan Jones (8)   105
Imaani Thomas & Kate Jones (8)   105
Georgia Tinton (8)   106
Kieran Jones (7)   106
Ross Leighton (8)   107

Ysgol Cilcennin, Lampeter
Ben Harvey (7)   107
Benito Thomas Gilmore (10)   107
Natasha Pearce (8)   108
Dale Robert Firth (8)   108
Crystal Gina Gilmore (10)   108
Sioned Jones (8)   109
Nathaniel Sawyer (8)   109
Kimberley Reeves (7)   110
Ben Smithers (10)   110
Chloe Jones (9)   111

Ysgol Dyffryn Trannon, Trefeglwys
George Reynolds (7)   111
Josh Cotton (8)   111
Hermia Hayward (7)   112
Jake Tranter (8)   112
Rebecca Cotton (7)   112
Zoé Jones (9)   113
Mia Maeér-Butterworth (7)   113
Elisabeth Owen (10)   113
Kira Maeér-Butterworth (10)   114

Jasmine Evans (9)	114
Rachel Mills (9)	115
Tyler Thomas (8)	115
Edward Rhys Jones (11)	116
Daniel Regan (9)	116

Ysgol Glannau Gwaun, Fishguard

Callum Shaw (9)	116
Amy Jones (9)	117
Adam Charles Lewis (8)	117
Rowan Fawcett (8)	118
Rhys Shaw (7)	118
Kai Finley Spike Williams (8)	118
Kevin MacDonald (8)	119
Daniel Rhys Evans (9)	119
Luke Richard Parr (9)	120
Zoe Mary Hayes (7)	120
Isobel Vickers (7)	121
Sophie Jamieson (9)	121
Nia Tyrrell (9)	122
Michael Watson (8)	122
Molly-May Hughes (8)	123
Thomas O'Sullivan (8)	123
Zara Thomas (9)	124
Abigail Hruzik (9)	124

Ysgol Gymraeg Bro Ogwr, Bridgend

Rhiannon Warren-Hopkin (7)	124
Jac Talbot (7)	125
Lucy Jane Crocker (7)	125
Alyssa Davies (7)	126
Phoebe Ann Lewis (7)	126
Bronwyn Siân Lewis (8)	126
Natalia Saman (8)	127
Chloe Harries (7)	127
Cari Haf Jones (7)	128
Ifan Lewis (7)	128
Cary Davies (7)	129
Imogen Elyse Hunt (7)	129
Eleri Ann Lewis (7)	130
Megan Lois Stephens (7)	130

Tomos Rhys Morgan (9)	131
Elen Lloyd (8)	131
Solomon Evans (8)	132
Rhodri Lewis (8)	132
Hannah Steele (9)	132
Sophie Davies (8)	133
Jordan (8)	133
Hannah Jones (9)	134
Brittany Wilson (8)	134
Llio Alaw Arfona Roberts (8)	135
Nathan Watts (8)	135
Nia Roberts (8)	136
Gruffydd Davies (8)	136
Cian Griffiths (8)	137
Gwennan Jenkin (9)	137
Keelan Birch (8)	138
Rhys Huw Muzzupappa (8)	138
Richard John Hughes (9)	138
Kairan Trebble (7)	139
Elliot Thomas (9)	139
Lowri Urquhart (8)	139
John-Michael Wilkes (8)	140
Llewellyn Mercelsanca (8)	140
Curtis David (9)	141
Cerys Siân Evans (8)	141

The Poems

Aberaeron - Our Town

Our town -
By the vast sea
Of grey, brown waves
Rough, high waves with white horses
Flat and smooth
With soft, blue, calm, gentle waves

Our town -
With the River Aeron
And its ducks which swim and paddle
And quack peacefully
Fast flowing over waterfalls
On its way to the sea

Our town -
Its benefactor, Alban Thomas Jones Gwynne
Who built the harbour
The straight streets and roads
The colourful houses of pink, purple, blue, yellow
Ty Stamp

Our town -
Is today cheerful and busy
With its cars and buses
The helpful people
Shops and facilities
People coming here on holiday
Exciting places and events
Cob festival, carnival, fair
A fun place to be
Exactly what we want

Our town!

Class Poem (Years 3 & 4)
Aberaeron Primary School, Aberaeron

Aberaeron Sea

The sea blue
The waves bash on the rocks
While the sun rises
The water gets smoother and smoother
While the water runs through the rocks
The fish swim through the calm sea
The sea wets the stones
Big and small
Grey, brown, black, yellow, orange
Purple, red and pink
Blue, silver and gold
Pebbles as smooth as carpet
The boats go up and down
When the sea is rough you can hear
The ringing of the boats
The seagulls fly over the ocean

On the beach
The children play happily
The jellyfish swim up and down.

Megan Hawkins (7), Nadine Owens & Tristan Williams (8), Ifan & Megan Davies (9)
Aberaeron Primary School, Aberaeron

Aberaeron

Shops, church, boats, chapels, schools,
Beach, sea and harbour
The big, fresh sea
Where colourful fish swim and swim

Above the smooth, calm sea
Seagulls swoop and squawk

The church and chapels
Are quiet places
To pray to God

The park, a good place to play
The library, a peaceful place to read
The school, a place to learn and concentrate
The shops - perfect places to buy food and souvenirs

The houses, so colourful
They stand out
Every time you look at them

Aberaeron has everything we want!

Emily Harwood, Bethany Hughes, Thomas & Liam
Aberaeron Primary School, Aberaeron

Our Seaside At Aberaeron

The big sea
So calm,
So peaceful,
White horses on the waves.
The River Aeron
Ducks swimming, paddling, quacking
Ducklings following
On the river
On the way down to the big sea.

The houses are colourful
As the stained-glass windows in the church
The beach is very rocky
White pebbles, orange pebbles, grey pebbles.
The church
A silent place to pray in
The busy council
Looks after the town.

Alban Thomas Jones Gwynne gave money
To build the harbour
So they named the square after him -
Sgwâr Alban
The large park by the River Aeron
Parc y Fro
Is big and fun to play in.

The Celtic sells great chips, cod and sausages
Aeron Coast's Garage
Is very kind and helpful.

Bleddyn Thomas, Erin McCudden & Beth Davies & Ryan
Aberaeron Primary School, Aberaeron

Aberaeron - A Good Place!

Streets wide
Houses colourful
In stormy weather
The river is rough
With big waves crashing to the sea

At school we learn
At home we rest
Ducks go *quack* on the River Aeron
Town hall clock goes *dong-dong*
The hairdresser goes *snip, snip, snip*

Hotels are good for staying the night
Boats in the harbour rock when the wind whistles
The boat bells *ding-a-ling*

The harbour waves crash on the rocks
When the waves go back
The rocks look as if they are rolling

A bank with lots of money
The chlorine smell of the swimming pool

Aberaeron is a good place!

Sara Williams (7), Hannah, Tia Norris (9) & Jordan
Aberaeron Primary School, Aberaeron

A Witch's Evil Poison

Thunder, lightning, my face so frightening,
Green and slimy and oh, so grimy!

A ripped dragon wing
And a crocodile's eye,
A bird that cannot sing
And a bat that cannot fly.

A round, fat rat
And warm, thick blood,
Spider's legs
And the scream of Robin Hood.

Thunder, lightning, my face so frightening,
Green and slimy and oh, so grimy!

Old lady's false teeth
And pig's sticky snot,
A hair of an armpit,
It really smells a lot!

Slimy bird poo
And naughty children's tongues,
The heart of a pig
And a dentist's lungs.

Thunder, lightning, my face so frightening,
Green and slimy and oh, so grimy!

Warm, thick blood
And a mouse's tail,
A leg of a cat
And an old, grubby wedding veil.

Carys Rees (9)
Croesty Primary School, Pencoed

Secret Spell

Stirling, whirling,
My tummy's turning,
At the sight of the cauldron burning.

Warm, thick blood
And slimy bird's poo,
Crocodile's eye
And old tadpoles in a shoe.

Cold rice pudding,
In a haunted house,
Something ate it,
It was a round, fat mouse.

Stirling, whirling,
My tummy's turning,
At the sight of the cauldron burning.

Ripped dragon's wing,
A witch's wart,
Rat's tail
And wolves, they like to stalk.

Badger's leg,
Owl's beak,
The witches were shocked,
The crow speaks.

Stirling, whirling,
My tummy's turning,
At the sight of the cauldron burning.

Ella Griffiths (8)
Croesty Primary School, Pencoed

Zombie Island

In my pot
I have got
A baby's diaper
And a windscreen wiper

Into my fire
I now must put
A rotten egg
And a smelly foot

Old man's pants
And dirty jeans
A rotten pancake
And cold baked beans

In my pot
I have got
A baby's diaper
And a windscreen wiper

One dead sheep
And a glass of wine
Some mouldy bread
And some fishing line

Ear of cat
And head of snake
One wasp sting
And half a gate

In my pot
I have got
A baby's diaper
And a windscreen wiper

One fish eye
And one dog's tail
A jug of blood
And one boiled snail

And don't forget
The king's heart
Or the lizard's tail
And put in a jam tart.

William Morgan (10)
Croesty Primary School, Pencoed

The Witches' Spell

A round, fat rat
And a stinky bat-faced mat
A scared cat
And a scared-looking hat.

Humble, bumble, stir up some crumble!

A lump of sticky pig's slime
Is enough to make my potion rot
Warm, thick blood and . . .
All I need now, a little cobwebbed slot.

Humble, bumble, stir up some crumble!

A bird's slimy beak
And a ripped dragon's wing
Some blood down a loo
And a girl who can't sing.

Humble, bumble, stir up some crumble!

Hair of an armpit
Some snake's fresh guts
Crocodile's eye and . . .
Some rotten nuts!

Amy Field (9)
Croesty Primary School, Pencoed

The Worst Witch Ever!

Double, bubble
Look at the time
Let's put in some slugs and slime!

Gooey fish eyes
And fluffy owl's wing
Slimy apple pips
And a haunted doorbell ring.

Rotten tomato
Chicken's blood
The head of a baby
That the mother loved.

Double, bubble
Look at the time
Let's put in some slugs and slime!

A mouldy carrot
A smile of a newborn baby
A sheep's trotter
And a hat of a very happy lady.

Snake's poison
A whisker off a kitten
Lion's nails
And my grandma's old mitten.

Double, bubble
Look at the time
Let's put in some slugs and slime!

Megan Bosley (8)
Croesty Primary School, Pencoed

The Witch's Spell

Double, trouble, cauldron bubble
Cooking, looking for extra trouble!

Into my cauldron I will put
Slugs and snails
Puppy dogs' tails
And old ladies' nails.

Crunched eye of a frog
Dead leg of a bee
Children's noses
Smelly fish from the sea.

Double, trouble, cauldron bubble
Cooking, looking for extra trouble!

Wild wasp's sting
Smelly, rotten egg
Firework's flame
And a dead man's leg.

Leg of a dragon
Eye of a sheep
Rotten skull
And teeth from a lady who can't sleep.

Double, trouble, cauldron bubble
Cooking, looking for extra trouble!

Double, trouble, cauldron bubble
Cooking, looking for extra trouble!

Rhys Young
Croesty Primary School, Pencoed

The Witch's Spell!

Hubble, bubble, toyland trouble
Cooking pot stir up some trouble!

Into my pot
I must now fling
An eye of a sheep
And a blackbird's wing

Into my pot
I have got
A big black cat
And a wing of a bat

Into my fire
I must throw
Ink from a pen
And a witch's toe

Hubble, bubble, toyland trouble
Cooking pot stir up some trouble!

Lewis Smith (9)
Croesty Primary School, Pencoed

Boo!

Spear fear when the sky's not clear,
We'll take away the eyes of a window cleaner.

The magic words I will now say,
The foot of a rabbit, ever so grey
And muddle up the time of night and day.

A mouldy ball of modelling clay,
Also including someone called May,
I'll take away a baby's dummy
And make it cry, 'Oh, help me, Mummy!'

Spear fear when the sky's not clear,
We'll take away the eyes of a window cleaner.

Daniel Watkins (9)
Croesty Primary School, Pencoed

The Witch's Spell

Bubble, trouble, flying puddle
Now, my cooking pot
Stir up some trouble!

Into my pot now must go, toe of gorilla
And eye of goat
With some blood for flavour
And head of mouse

An eye of a girl
And a mouldy toenail
A slimy bug
With blue blood

Bubble, trouble, flying puddle
Now, my cooking pot
Stir up some trouble!

Sheepdog's tail
And blood of cat
A snail's slimy trail
And a dead rat

Rotten teeth
Upon the heath
I shall go
To gather green frogs' teeth

Bubble, trouble, flying puddle
Now, my cooking pot
Stir up some trouble!

Into my cauldron
I'm going to fling, eye of boy
I just love the next one
With a fairy wing.

Daniel Weeks (8)
Croesty Primary School, Pencoed

Midnight

Hubble, bubble, stir up some trouble
Add some poison and make some bubbles!

Sheep's eye
And an old man's toe,
A king's heart
And a rotten pie.

Now a jug of slime,
A dead rat
And a puppy's tail,
Eew! Look at the time!

Hubble, bubble, stir up some trouble
Add some poison and make some bubbles!

Into my pot
Is a horrible slug
And an ear of a girl,
A rib of a human
And one slimy bug.

Now a rat,
A dog's tongue
And dirty oil,
A wing of a bat,

Hubble, bubble, stir up some trouble
Add some poison and make some bubbles!

Emily Ames (9)
Croesty Primary School, Pencoed

The Witch's Bowl

Into my bowl
I must chuck in,
Zombie's heart and lion's mane
Or maybe a sardine tin.

Giraffe's tongue,
Spider's web,
Rabbit's droppings,
Old man's leg.

Abracadabra, allakazam! Hocus pocus, turn round!

Crabs' legs,
Fishes' scales,
Hair of an armpit,
Monkeys' tails.

Guts of a worm,
Bark of a tree,
Wing of a wasp,
Green seaweed.

Abracadabra, allakazam! Hocus pocus, turn round!

Abracadabra, allakazam!
Hocus pocus, turn round!
Abracadabra, allakazam!
Hocus pocus, where's your broom?

Josie Reffell (8)
Croesty Primary School, Pencoed

The Zombie's Spell

Mumble, jumble, with a bang,
Eye of cat and leg of man!

Into my brew there,
Now will be thrown,
A baby's diaper
And a slimy toe.

A goat's tail
And horse's poo
And just for special,
An old lady's loo.

Mumble, jumble, with a bang,
Eye of cat and leg of man!

One rotten pie
And a big toad head,
One more thing,
A cold boiled egg.

A fang of a wolf
And yet another egg
And one more thing,
Some mouldy bread.

Owain Hicks (8)
Croesty Primary School, Pencoed

The Witch's Spell!

Hocus pocus, allakazam
Old men's socks
And a smelly ram!

Into my pot
I'm going to throw
An eye of a boy
And an old man's toe

Hocus pocus, allakazam
Old men's socks
And a smelly ram!

A bulb of a light
And a pig's nose
And a rotten saucepan
And a rotten pear

Hocus pocus, allakazam
I'm going to throw
Old men's socks
And a smelly ram!

Ayesha Williams (9)
Croesty Primary School, Pencoed

Zombie Island

Hocus pocus, double lotus!

Into my cauldron
I'm going to put
A rotten frog
And a rotten apple

Old man's pants
And a dirty top
And rotten break
And Dad's Ready Brek

Hocus pocus, double lotus!

One dead hedgehog
And a dead zombie
And a honking toe

A stolen toe
And a stolen goat
And a jar of jam
And a glass of malt

Hocus pocus, double lotus!

Tail of rat
And paw of cat
Screams and shouts
From the haunted house

Do not forget a glass of squash
Oh, look at the time
We have to go
Bye-bye!

Hocus pocus, double lotus!

Tom Stride (9)
Croesty Primary School, Pencoed

Dizzle Dazzle

Hocus pocus, it's time to focus!

Into my pot
I'm going to toss
A witch's broom
And a cookery pot

Hocus-pocus, it's time to focus!

One dead fly
And a wild wasp's sting
An eye of a sheep
And the heart of a king

Hocus pocus, it's time to focus!

Ellie Woolhouse-Jones
Croesty Primary School, Pencoed

Boo!

Hubble, bubble
Make some trouble!

Old men's socks
And rabbit droppings
Fresh new bleach
And dirty jeans

Hubble, bubble
Make some trouble!

A bloody heart
And old ladies' socks
One dead fly
And a rotten egg!

Justine Stark (9)
Croesty Primary School, Pencoed

Boo!

Hocus pocus, turn around
Hocus pocus, touch the ground!

Into my cauldron
I'm going to throw
A rat's tail
And an old man's nail

Hocus pocus, turn around
Hocus pocus, touch the ground!

One dead bee
And a wild sting
An eye of a bird
And a witch's ring!

Megan Griffiths
Croesty Primary School, Pencoed

The Witch's Spell

Hubble, bubble
Stir up some trouble!

Witch's blood in a puddle
Big man's toe sitting there
Rats come out, eating hair!

Hubble, bubble
Stir up some trouble!

Crushed up toes
Lying there
Spider's guts, everywhere!

Jamie Dyer
Croesty Primary School, Pencoed

Midnight

Hubble, bubble, toilet trouble
Cooking pot stir up some trouble!

Into my pot
I now must fling
An eye of a sheep
And a thousand nits

Into my pot
I have got
A big black cat
And a wing of a bat

In my fire
I must desire
Red ink of a pen
And a witch's den

Hubble, bubble, toilet trouble
Cooking pot stir up some trouble!

Into my pot
I now must fling
An eye of a sheep
And a thousand nits

A wing of a wasp
A stinky brain
A monkey's bottom
And oil from a train

Hubble, bubble, toilet trouble
Cooking pot stir up some trouble!

Donovan Massebo (8)
Croesty Primary School, Pencoed

The Witch's Spell!

Hubble, bubble at the double
Cooking pot making trouble!

A pig's nose
Lion's teeth
Hair from an armpit
Rotten beef

Hubble, bubble at the double
Cooking pot making trouble!

Dog's tail
Zombie's eyes
A smelly, warm sock
And a rotten pie

Dirty pink cow's tongue
Blood out of a lizard
Smelly flies
A dirty, sticky wizard

Hubble, bubble at the double
Cooking pot making trouble!

A girl's toe
A baby's fingernail
Pink, dead worms
A dragon's tail

Hubble, bubble at the double
Cooking pot making trouble!

Katy Abbott
Croesty Primary School, Pencoed

Zombie Island

Abracadabra, allakazam
Make me a potion as fast as you can!

I will put in my fire
One dead frog
A slimy worm
And a snout from a hog

I will put in my fire
Dragon smoke
One snail's shell
And some Diet Coke

Abracadabra, allakazam
Make me a potion as fast as you can!

I will put in my fire
A leg of a frog
Old man's nose
Smelly socks
And little toes

I will put in my fire
One flat tyre
A dead leg
And some barbed wire

Abracadabra, allakazam
Make me a potion as fast as you can!

Sam Rowland-Jones (8)
Croesty Primary School, Pencoed

Witch's Spell

Hubble, bubble, jungle rumble
Cooking pot make some more trouble!

Into my cauldron
I'm going to throw
Some mouldy bread
And a dead crow

One dead fox
And a human eye
The heart of a dragon
And a slimy pie

Hubble, bubble, jungle rumble
Cooking pot make some more trouble!

Wing of a plane
Some brown snow
A mouldy pancake
And a muddy bow

One mouse head
And a flat bat
Car brake
And one fat cat

Hubble, bubble, jungle rumble
Cooking pot make some more trouble!

Hubble, bubble, jungle rumble
Cooking pot make some more trouble!

Hubble, bubble, jungle rumble
Cooking pot make some more trouble!

Joshua Brown (8)
Croesty Primary School, Pencoed

Boo!

Hubble, bubble
Stir up trouble
Chop that wood
Make it bubble

Into my pot
I now must throw
A rotten pancake
And frog toes

Into my fire
I'm going to throw
A rotten pancake
And smelly toes

Hubble, bubble
Stir up trouble
Chop that wood
Make it bubble

Dead rabbit, slimy worms
And a rat's tail
A big spider
And soggy bird poo

Hubble, bubble
Stir up trouble
Chop that wood
Make it bubble!

Chris Cooper (9)
Croesty Primary School, Pencoed

Dizzle, Dazzle

Mumble, jumble, stir up some thunder
One tail of a mouse
Two heads from owls
Three legs from a frog
And lips of a king
One fly
Two parakeets
Six eyes
For a surprise!

Mumble, jumble, stir up some thunder
Now I can throw in
A witch's ring
A little girl's freckle
An old woman's wrinkle
A dolphin's voice
A bit of sheep fur
And the sound of blood
Running through a little girl's thumb!

Mumble, jumble, stir up some thunder!

Leah Eyre (9)
Croesty Primary School, Pencoed

Fear

Fear is a white cold shiver down your back
Fear is the darkness of the night, silent and heartless
Fear talks to me in my head, giving me nightmares
Making me scream, following me wherever I go
Fear is bitter, so biter that you can't speak
Don't look for fear
You won't find it
It's living inside you.

Saffron Foster (9)
Croesty Primary School, Pencoed

Fear

Fear,
Black like the midnight sky
Shadowing over the moonlight,
Fear,
Smells of a bag of rubbish
Rotting in the miserable dump,
Fear,
Tastes horrible and slimy
Like a sticky frog dripping with duckweed,
Fear,
Screams like a girl
In a gloomy forest,
Fear,
Cold and wet
Like an ice cube,
Fear,
It lives in your . . .
Dark . . . dark . . . mind!

Cerys Bethan Dyke (9)
Croesty Primary School, Pencoed

Fear

The sky was blood-red
Fear hung in the air
It went through me
The air was cold
A wolf was howling
Slow, long footsteps
Banging
My spine wriggling
Slowly fainting to the floor!
Awwwoooo!

Alex Wilson (9)
Croesty Primary School, Pencoed

Hallowe'en Scare

Hallowe'en
Through the night,
Everything
Is fear and fright!

Eye of cat
And toe of frog,
A soggy newt
From a murky bog.

Now here come
The fumes of smoke,
Rising up
To make you choke!

Hallowe'en
Through the night,
Everything
Is fear and fright!

Jellyfish sting
And dragon's fin
Eagle wing
And earthworms sing!

Hallowe'en
Through the night,
Everything
Is fear and fright!

Jamie Powell (8)
Croesty Primary School, Pencoed

Bwgan Wood

Big, dark, creaky trees
Reaching out at you.
Walking through this forest
Isn't a trip to the zoo.
Dark shadows round every corner
Listen, can you hear the poisons brewing?
Oh, come on! Please stop chewing your fingernails!
Look! Over there!
What is it?
Where has it come from?
It's small and black
Fat and round
It's starting to run
It's getting closer
It's here!
Aaarrrrrggghhhh!
Where am I?
Will I die or am I dead?
Why is it so dark?
Argh! Something poked me!
I think it left a mark
I'm all alone
With no one to talk to
But myself
The big question is
How long will I be here?
Only time can tell.

Ellyn Williams (9)
Croesty Primary School, Pencoed

My Gran!

My gran is
Kind, gentle and generous.
My gran has
Soft, white, curly hair.
My gran has
A bent back and wrinkly skin.
My gran is
Very fragile, like a china doll.
My gran
Does everything slowly.
My gran
Loves to sleep and drink cups of tea.
My gran
Is now in Heaven!

Zoe Morgan (10)
Croesty Primary School, Pencoed

Bwgan Wood

Within the darkness of Bwgan Wood
Trees come alive,
Staggering branches reaching out at all,
Who pass by, whether short or tall.

Within the ground of Bwgan Wood
Howling winds
Blow off all the leaves.

Within the shadows of Bwgan Wood
Creepy creatures loom between the trees,
Whoever passes by, they tease.

Within the paths of Bwgan Wood
Dull plants roam all around,
Moon gleaming down.

Sarah Davies (9)
Croesty Primary School, Pencoed

Fear

Fear is the colour of blood-red
Dripping from a vampire's fangs
It smells like sweat
Running down your face
And it also smells
Like bad breath
So hold your nose
If you're near someone scared
You hear a scream
And then a shout so loud
You're looking where it comes from
You feel afraid
Scared and alone
Fear lives in your body
And all around you
But it's invisible.

Megan Owen (9)
Croesty Primary School, Pencoed

Bwgan Wood

The brown, creepy branches,
Grabbing out,
I started to run
And started to shout.

The glittering moonlight,
Showed us the way,
It seemed like forever,
But was only a day.

The monster was just above my head,
I heard a loud scream,
I'd rather be dead!

Joshua Maunder (9)
Croesty Primary School, Pencoed

Fear

Fear is the colour of dull, dim, blood-red
That could only be found
In the depths of your body.

It looks like a deserted swamp
With trees whispering like a child talking a secret
That doesn't want to be told.

Fear tastes like drinking a cup of blood
With spiders and cockroaches
Crawling up the side of the glass!

It's like being ice
Because it is so damp and cold
But the worst thing is
That it's like a deadly man rising from his gravestone.

Fear sounds like rain
Thundering down like a drum of death.

It feels like a spider's crawling up your frozen, stiff back
You're so alarmed, that your face is as pale as a ghost
And it feels as though someone is ready to snatch you.

You can't see fear, because it lives deep in you.

That's what I call fear!

Taylor Johnson (9)
Croesty Primary School, Pencoed

My Granny

My granny has grey and white hair
She walks around with a bent back
And likes to watch horse races.

She likes to have cups of tea
And sit in a big chair
And she likes watching the birds in the garden.

Harry Lock (9)
Croesty Primary School, Pencoed

Gerald

He's a warm-hearted but lonely man,
Very old and quite wrinkly,
But inside, he's the youngest I've seen,
He likes wearing very loud T-shirts,
Which make me laugh!
The nice thing about him is,
He likes squeezing my hand
And hugging me *hard!*
Every day when we pick him up,
We drop him off at the pub sometimes,
To meet his jolly good friends,
He looks after me as if I were his own
And I love him very much!

Elinor Taylor (9)
Croesty Primary School, Pencoed

Nanna Sylvia

My nan, when she kisses me, her lips vibrate
She's cold and loved.
She's kind and friendly,
She watches me play.
She clicks back and thinks about when she could play.
Her hands are chalky-white,
She has got glittery white hair.
My nan moves really slowly
Because she's got a few brittle bones
And she's a bit shaky.
My nan wear glasses
Because her eyes are blurry.
She forgets things and we giggle,
My nan is nice.

Olivia Bruford (9)
Croesty Primary School, Pencoed

Bwgan Woods

Bwgan Woods
Dark, cold
Things moving all about
Creaking trees
Arms grabbing out
To get you
Shadows moving
You're not moving
Trying to find
Out who's there
There are things
That are there
You're not alone
You're with someone
But you don't know it
You know there
Are creatures there
Just to warn you
They are hungry creatures
So . . .

Watch out!

Lauren Sproul (10)
Croesty Primary School, Pencoed

Fear

Fear is blood-red
Smelling like danger
Tasting of horror
And sounding like a wolf howling
It looks like death
And it also lives in midnight madness
I had fear.

Corey Jeffrey Jones (10)
Croesty Primary School, Pencoed

Bwgan Wood

Trees with bent backs
Hands reaching out
Nothing to do
Nothing to see
Except the moonlight
Shadows all around

A shiver up my spine
The angry face of the moon staring down
I look up at the clouds
Now fading
Almost invisible
Skipping from tree to tree

In pitch-black
I see something move
A black crow flutters out of the trees
No way out!

Benjamin Davies (9)
Croesty Primary School, Pencoed

Impressions Of Bwgan Wood

Trees swaying back and forth
Fiercely in the howling wind

Shadows of creatures lurking
In the middle of the stormy night

Eyes hiding
In the rustling brambles

The moon grinning
Branches grabbing.

Nia Weston (9)
Croesty Primary School, Pencoed

Bwgan Woods

In Bwgan Woods
Shadows creep everywhere
To get you
Like hands grabbing you
Leaves rustling
Creepy laughter from the sky
Running, coming from the ground
Holes coming from nowhere
Creatures popping out
Just about to get *you!*
People walking through
The woods thinking
They're done
But they're not
Spiky plants growing
Faster and faster
Starting to wrap
Round and round
Your arms and legs
Don't go into Bwgan Woods
At night-time
Alone!

Nicole Sproul (10)
Croesty Primary School, Pencoed

My Old Bampy

My old bampy is as old as can be,
He has crow's feet eyes,
A beard and moustache.
He has scruffy hair and is shaky.
He has a hearing aid and false teeth
And is always asleep,
But when he laughs,
He is as young as can be!

Emily Sims (9)
Croesty Primary School, Pencoed

I Hope You Are Ill

I hope you are ill,
I hope you are ill,
If you're not ill,
This potion will spill!

In the house mice go round,
Steal their tails,
Bring them down!

I hope you are ill,
I hope you are ill,
If you're not ill,
This potion will spill!

On the farm you must take,
A rat so small,
A big fat snake.

I hope you are ill,
I hope you are ill,
If you're not ill,
This potion will spill!

Matthew Cowell (8)
Croesty Primary School, Pencoed

Nan

My nan is fun and kind to me
She is a great nan to me
She spoils me with nice things to eat
She is not strong or weak
She is my great nan
She is a bit wrinkly
She wears glasses when she reads
Her hearing is going
She is the best nan in the world.

Elliot Clegg (9)
Croesty Primary School, Pencoed

An Old Person

Little Roy Keeling,
Is so very appealing,
He's very wrinkly
And his eyes are twinkly.

He breathes like Darth Vader,
From Venezuela,
He is really fun,
Because he wants to be young.

He likes pasta,
Cooked even faster,
He likes cups of tea,
But best of all . . .
He likes me!

James Cattermole (9)
Croesty Primary School, Pencoed

Evil Death

A wicked witch's harp
Runner beans, flat
Wooden broomstick, sharp
Pointy black hat.

Wings of a bat
Brown ants' legs
Witch's evil cat
Stinging scorpion eggs.

A wicked witch's harp
Runner beans, flat
Wooden broomstick, sharp
Pointy black hat.

Thomas Pound (9)
Croesty Primary School, Pencoed

Old People

Old people are wrinkly and weak
And they aren't very strong
Old people look tired
And they have a slight pong!
Old people tell tales of their past lives
And sing songs.

Old people can be a bit deaf
Or are unable to see
Old people sometimes drink loads of tea
And always seem to need a wee!

Old people at times look sad
With eyes set deep
Old people may need a stick
As they find walking a feat.

Old people often need
To have much more sleep
Old people look funny
With pink gums instead of teeth.

Old people have grey hair
Or sometimes are bald
But never mind the above
We still love them all!

Samuel Mark Bontempo (10)
Croesty Primary School, Pencoed

Fear

Fear of a dark green swamp sinking
Smell of rotten bananas goes up your nose
Echoing noise like dishes clanging
You have a *big* fear and a graveyard with switching tombs.

Ellis Griffiths (9)
Croesty Primary School, Pencoed

Witch's Spell

Hallowe'en is coming,
You'd better start to run,
Witch's spells are in the air,
Watch out everyone!

Into my pot goes,
Eye of a pig,
Hair of a wig,
Dog that cannot dig.

Hallowe'en is coming,
You'd better start to run,
Witch's spells are in the air,
Watch out everyone!

A dead bird's wing,
Put in a dog's jaw,
Jewel of a king
And a brown bear's paw.

Emily Smith (8)
Croesty Primary School, Pencoed

Bwgan Wood

Explorers looking suspicious
At mysterious footsteps
Behind them
And the trees rustling around them.

The strange shadows
Shining down at them
So weird those shadows were.

Trees twitching
Leaves coming down, one by one
Trees swaying back and forth
Moving suspiciously.

Ryan Frewen (9)
Croesty Primary School, Pencoed

Brain Of A Bird

Eyelashes, tongue,
Fingers and lung,
Makes a good spell,
To simmer and smell.

Brain of a bird,
A fiery nerd,
Black cow's dung,
A warthog's snort.

Root of foxglove,
Tail of a whale,
Head of a fish,
Shell of a snail.

Eyelashes, tongue,
Fingers and lung,
Makes a good spell,
To simmer and smell.

Jacob Hughes
Croesty Primary School, Pencoed

My Nan

My nan is quite old
She likes to go shopping with her friends
She comes over to our house
And gives me big hugs
Which can lift me off the floor
She sometimes forgets things that I have told her
We have a dog called Rosie
And my nan plays with her all the time
She likes to go on holiday
But whether she's home or away
She will always think about me
And never forget me at anytime.

Alex King (9)
Croesty Primary School, Pencoed

The Witch's Spell

Hallowe'en is coming
So you'd better start to run!
The witches are coming
For everyone!

Eye of frog,
Toe of bat,
Leg of rat
And that is that!

Hallowe'en is coming
For everyone!
The witches and the black cats
Are nearly here!

Thumb of man,
Wing of ghost,
Leg of dog
And head of cat.

Hallowe'en is coming
So you'd better start to run!

Abbey Griffiths (8)
Croesty Primary School, Pencoed

Old People

John, my next door neighbour
He's old and does sports
He likes cycling
And is a member of a club
He likes all sport
John loves his garden
Plus his tortoises
Who cares if he's retired?
I think he's cool!

Callum Sparks (9)
Croesty Primary School, Pencoed

Slimy Cats With Big Fat Rats

Slimy potion
Dirty old lotion
Mixing, stirring
Kitty cats purring

Smelly old frogs
Deadly dogs
Big fat rats
Stinky old cats

Slimy potion
Dirty old lotion
Mixing, stirring
Kitty cats purring.

Kitty cats' pins,
Dirty old bins,
Fishes' fins
Zombies' skins.

Dylan Barrett (8)
Croesty Primary School, Pencoed

My Dadcu

My dadcu is old and growing bald,
When he touches you, it's like he's been in the shower too long,
Dadcu has a nice smile,
He's kind, joyful and funny,
The best part is when he wobbles his tummy
And he plays golf,
Sadly, he's as wrinkly as a prune,
He always sings a jolly tune,
He's travelled almost all over the world,
Too bad my dadcu is not as jolly as a clown
But laughs like Santa, even in town.

Rosie Thomas (9)
Croesty Primary School, Pencoed

Smelly Mould And Freezing Cold

Smelly mould and freezing cold,
Let's get the children, good as gold.

Root of tree,
Tail of dog,
Stem of ivy,
Tongue of frog.

Chicken's eyeball,
Chocolate spread,
Children's heads,
Mouldy bread.

Smelly mould and freezing cold,
Lets get the children, good as gold.

Joe Thomas (8)
Croesty Primary School, Pencoed

Fear!

Fear is the colour of midnight-grey
And everybody feels it in their own little way
To me it tastes like foul dripping sweat!
As if a smelly sock has been in something wet
It sounds like a black, unhappy dog crying
As if it can see or hear something dying
It feels like the hardest, sharpest spike
Like the spokes that are broken on my bike
I'm glad that fear lives in the sea
Cos I feel washed out when it comes through me.

Liam Bowen (9)
Croesty Primary School, Pencoed

Mixing And Stirring

Mixing and stirring,
Mixing and stirring,
The witches never stop,
To keep the cauldron burning.
Rat's eye,
Cat's eye,
Jiggling squid
And bats flying by.
Fierce lion's roar,
Elephant's quiver,
Wild boar,
Large giant's shiver.
Mixing and stirring,
Mixing and stirring,
The witches never stop,
To keep the cauldron burning.
Bat's head,
Scorpion's legs,
Cats called Ned
And weird eggs.
Slimy ghouls,
Broken rules,
Stinky fouls,
Sparkly rules.

Rhyse Edwards (8)
Croesty Primary School, Pencoed

Horrible Witches

Horrible witches
Fly up high,
Up into
The cool night sky.

Puppy eyes
And dog cries,
Nail of cat
And a great big hat.

Hair of bear
In our lair,
Magic pot
You hold a lot!

Horrible witches
Fly up high,
Up into
The cool night sky.

Rotten leaves
And mushy peas,
A squashy snake
From a muddy lake.

A claw of an adder
Rung of a ladder,
A sting of a bee
Head of a flea.

Chloe Chilcott (9)
Croesty Primary School, Pencoed

Rats' Tails

Rats' tails,
Witches' nails,
Mix together,
To make some quails.
Beetles black,
Make a tasty snack,
Potions, potions,
That's the notion.
Rats' tails,
Witches' nails,
Mix together,
To make some quails.
Cold, hairy,
Rotten mice,
Slimy squids
And fluffy tights.
Rats' tails
Witches' nails,
Mix together,
To make some quails.
Furry bats black,
Make a tasty snack,
Smelly cats
And horrible hats.

Ben Gwyther (8)
Croesty Primary School, Pencoed

Deadly Spell

Bats, bats,
Like to scare rats,
Dogs, dogs,
Like to chase frogs.

Cow's eye,
A hairy fly,
Woodlice blood,
Slimy slug.

Bats, bats,
Like to scare rats,
Dogs, dogs,
Like to chase frogs.

Lizard's tail,
An old oak tree,
Mixed together
With bluebell tea.

Bats, bats,
Like to scare rats,
Dogs, dogs,
Like to chase frogs.

Paw of a bear,
Foot of a bat,
A slimy slug hat,
An ugly cat.

Bats, bats,
Like to scare rats,
Dogs, dogs,
Like to chase frogs.

Liver of a pig,
Tail of a cat,
Heart of a queen,
Nose of a rat.

Emily Coles (7)
Croesty Primary School, Pencoed

Horrible Poem

We are making a spell
To do you harm
So to keep you safe
You'd better make a charm

Ear of pig
Tail of bug
Leg of sheep
Eye of slug

We are making a spell
To do you harm
So to keep you safe
You'd better make a charm

Lip of frog
Claw of dog
Heart of snake
Tongue of hog

We are making a spell
To do you harm
So to keep you safe
You'd better make a charm

Paw of a bear
Foot of a cat
A dog's hair
And a witch's hat

We are making a spell
To do you harm
So to keep you safe
You'd better make a charm

Leaf of ivy
Root of bluebell
Stem of rose
In it goes.

Charlotte Morgan (8)
Croesty Primary School, Pencoed

Frogs And Snails, Witch's Nails

Frogs' eyeballs,
Tummy of a king,
Black hole of a snake,
Electric eel's sting.

Frogs and snails,
Witch's nails,
Owls' tails,
Never fails!

Heart of vampire,
Fur of a dog,
Pint of blood,
Eyebrow of frog.

Frogs and snails,
Witch's nails,
Owls' tails,
Never fails!

Bone of skeleton,
Claw of a crow,
Head of a bird,
Grasshopper's toe.

Frogs and snails,
Witch's nails,
Owls' tails,
Never fails!

Bat's head,
Rotten bread,
Smelly eggs,
Frogs' legs.

Scott Brown (8)
Croesty Primary School, Pencoed

Beware!

Hallowe'en is coming,
So we eat our liver
And if you touch it,
You will shiver!

Doggy eyes
And broken thighs,
Mix the pot,
It makes it hot.

Here come the bats,
We sacrifice our cats,
Goblin's blood,
That made the flood.

Hallowe'en is coming
So we eat our liver
And if you touch it,
You will shiver!

Human's head
And rotten bread,
Smelly frogs
And deadly dogs.

Slithering snakes
And a witch who bakes,
A tongue of a cat
And a big, scary bat.

Hallowe'en is coming,
So we eat our liver
And if you touch it,
You will shiver!

Rhys Butler (8)
Croesty Primary School, Pencoed

Do Not Enter!

Hallowe'en is coming
And the children will be out
I will be taking one
So they'd better watch out!

The blood of a bunny
A nerd so funny
And a rotten egg so runny.

Hallowe'en is coming
And the children will be out
I will be taking one
So they'd better watch out!

Now into my pot
With a terrible splash
The brain of a bird
Lightning flash.

Hallowe'en is coming
And the children will be out
I will be taking one
So they'd better watch out!

Slimy pig's ear
Dry lion's eye
And a slice of pie!

Kieran Parrish
Croesty Primary School, Pencoed

Freaky Spell

Witch's eyes,
Witch's thighs,
Witch's hair,
Witch's stare.

Honey bees,
Mixed with keys,
Monkey's tail
And icy hail.

Witch's eyes,
Witch's thighs,
Witch's hair,
Witch's stare.

Slimy, slithery frogs,
Nasty, growling dogs,
Hard, round stones,
Smooth, round bones.

Witch's eyes,
Witch's thighs,
Witch's hair,
Witch's stare.

Joshua
Croesty Primary School, Pencoed

Potions

Witches here!
Witches there!
Witches, witches
Everywhere!

Eye of a human,
Wing of bat,
Hump of camel,
Hair of a cat.

Horn of a rhino,
Moo of a cow,
Tail of a puppy dog,
That's a lot, *wow!*

Witches here!
Witches there!
Witches, witches
Everywhere!

Mouldy soap,
Hair of a child,
Slimy jellyfish,
That has turned mild.

Witches here!
Witches there!
Witches, witches
Everywhere!

Natalie Richards (7)
Croesty Primary School, Pencoed

Brain Of Bug

Stir it, stir it, to make it stink!
Stir it, stir it, to make them drink!

Brain of bug
Slime of slug
Eye of newt
A puppy so cute.

Heart of toad
A sack of hair
Give some kids
A terrible scare!
Boo!

Stir it, stir it, to make it stink!
Stir it, stir it, to make them drink!

Hair of a hare
Spine of an elephant
An eye of a bear
An ear of a deer.

A piece of glass
Half a skull
A dead man's bone
And a leg of a gull.
And a tooth of a wolf

Stir it, stir it, to make it stink!
Stir it, stir it, to make them drink!

Dylan Grey
Croesty Primary School, Pencoed

I Hate Witches Because . . .

Stirring, stirring, keep on stirring,
Keep the boiling water whirring,
Doggies yelping, kittens purring,
Don't watch too long or your eyes will start blurring!

Boiling bogies out of an owl's nose,
Now he can't smell the scent of a rose,
A monkey's tail chopped in half,
You will always hear his deadly laugh.

Stirring, stirring, keep on stirring,
Keep the boiling water whirring,
Doggies yelping, kittens purring,
Don't watch too long or your eyes will start blurring!

Lots of birds,
Mixed with rotten curds,
Tails of lizards,
Mixed with wizards.

Stirring, stirring, keep on stirring,
Keep the boiling water whirring,
Doggies yelping, kittens purring,
Don't watch too long or your eyes will start blurring!

Hair of a vicious bear
And a sign saying *'beware!'*
A crazy boar
And a wild lion's roar.

Stirring, stirring, keep on stirring,
Keep the boiling water whirring,
Doggies yelping, kittens purring,
Don't watch too long or your eyes will start blurring!

Now our wicked spell is done,
No more children on the run,
Hickle, hackle, boil and bubble,
Watch out boys, here comes trouble!
Ha! Ha! Ha!

Cameron Fyvie-Davies (8)
Croesty Primary School, Pencoed

Witch's Spells

Dog's paw,
Tiger's claw,
Panther's jaw
And lion's roar.

Frogs and snails,
White rats' tails,
Witch's spells,
Will not fail!

Lizard lips,
Furry flies,
Puppy, kitten,
Old sea's eyes.

Frogs and snails,
White rats' tails,
Witch's spells,
Will not fail!

Crocodile's snap,
An old white rat,
A black and white cat
And that is that!

Frogs and snails,
White rats' tails,
Witch's spells,
Will not fail!

Stinky rats,
Ugly bats,
A spotty cat
And that is that!

Shereen Miers (8)
Croesty Primary School, Pencoed

Zoe's Spooky Poem

Be wise or they will take your eyes,
Then tell you terrible, spooky lies.

The witches on broomsticks flying around,
Frightening the children on the ground,
Ha, ha, ha, hee, hee, hee,
I'll eat your children for my tea.

Be wise or they will take your eyes,
Then tell you terrible, spooky lies.

I'll mix up your eyes and your spotty nose,
In the cauldron it all goes,
Eating your fingers, biting your toes,
Stirring the cauldron whilst nibbling your nose.

Be wise or they will take your eyes,
Then tell you terrible, spooky lies.

Keeping the frogs in my witch's hat,
Looking after Spooky, my big, black cat,
Stirring the potions and lotions with my broomstick,
Oh, how I feel such a wicked, evil witch!

Be wise or they will take your eyes,
Then tell you terrible, spooky lies.

All ghosts and ghouls flying around,
Scaring people in Pencoed Town,
Trick or treating all night long,
Knocking on doors, ringing the bell - *ding-dong!*

Zoe Jones (8)
Croesty Primary School, Pencoed

Hallowe'en Is Coming

Frogs and dogs,
Inside my pot,
Big enough,
To stir the lot.

Monkey's tail
And hoof of deer,
Inside the cauldron
Will appear.

Frogs and dogs,
Inside my pot,
Big enough,
To stir the lot.

Slug's slime,
Dragonfly eye,
Snail's shell
And eagle's cry.

Frogs and dogs,
Inside my pot,
Big enough,
To stir the lot.

Screaming cats,
All the cold beans,
Flapping bats,
Make them scream!

Geddy Nash
Croesty Primary School, Pencoed

Rotten Pear In The Pot

Dirty rats scurrying round
And one egg that weighs a pound.

Skin of rotten pear
A diamond that is rare.

Dirty rats scurrying round
And one egg that weighs a pound.

A wild boar's claw
A carrot that is raw.

Dirty rats scurrying round
And one egg that weighs a pound!

Liam Hiett (7)
Croesty Primary School, Pencoed

Hallowe'en Night

At night it is very frightening,
At night there's thunder and lightning.

A slimy, slippery snake,
A dead fish from the black lake,
The heart of a bird,
Get this potion stirred.

At night it is very frightening,
At night there's thunder and lightning.

A slippery worm,
The sting from a bumblebee,
Mice screech and squirm,
Take a look and see . . .

Dylan Davies
Croesty Primary School, Pencoed

Gymnastics

I love gymnastics,
I love to bounce,
I spring and spring
And I like to pounce.

I go on the box, the beam and bars
And if I could, I'd jump to the stars,
I run and run and have lots of fun,
I get so busy, I really go dizzy.

I like to go on the bars,
I like to go on the floor,
I like to go on the beam and vault
And I always come back for more.

Cartwheels, flicks, forward rolls,
Backflip pike, backward rolls,
Ribbons, balls, hoola-hoops,
I get tangled in these loops.

Mats, mats, so need mats,
If we don't, we will collapse,
Sparkly leotards everywhere,
Shorts, tracksuits, tied-back hair.

Now it's time to cool down,
Gently jog and move around,
Until we go the next day,
When I'll run and jump and leap and play,
Tired, weary, we make our way.

Beatrice Angharad Wynne Edwards (11)
Llangeitho Primary School, Tregaron

The Seasons

In the winter months
We shelter from the cold,
We would hate to get sick,
So we do as we are told.

We wear our coats and mittens,
We wear our hats and scarves
And if at night we're chilly,
We have relaxing baths.

But then the winter slips away
And snowdrops will appear,
Growing in every garden
And in every field near.

The spring is at last among us,
With lovely blossoming trees
And birds flying swiftly,
In the gentle breeze.

The days are getting longer,
The summer's finally here,
School is now over,
'Hooray!' the children cheer.

The beaches are chock-a-block,
The swimming pool is full,
The kids are playing tug-of-war,
So come on people, pull!

Now it is the autumn,
The harvest's getting near,
With enough food for the animals
And every village here.

But now don't think the end is near,
Because the seasons will be back next year.

Catrin Pink (11)
Llangeitho Primary School, Tregaron

Big Fat Billy

Big fat Billy,
Thought that healthy eating was silly,
He ate loads of junk,
While listening to hip-hop funk.

Big fat Billy would say,
What's for breakfast today?
Sugar, cream and Coco Pops,
Followed by twirly, whirly lollipops.

Billy loved crisps, biscuits and sweets,
He wouldn't eat grains or wheat,
Gulping, stuffing and slurping,
Then a whole load of burping.

Big fat Billy never went out,
Because he was so very stout,
He always watched TV,
What a sight to see!

Big fat Billy couldn't run
And one morning, he decided that wasn't much fun,
So at lunch that day,
The crisps, biscuits and sweets he threw away.

One afternoon, big fat Billy read,
That it was good to eat fresh fruit and brown bread,
He decided to give it a try
And after a week he felt so good! My, oh my!

Billy's going to be a healthy boy,
Unlike a big, fat, cuddly toy,
He's not big fat Billy anymore,
But fit, fierce Billy, once and for all!

Caitlin Culyer (9)
Llangeitho Primary School, Tregaron

Please, Mum!

'Please, please, Mum,' I said,
As I sat on my bed.
'All I want for a present,
Is nothing unpleasant.
Just a small pup,
That might fit in a cup.
It doesn't have to be big,
Or as tall as a pig.
It doesn't have to be fat,
Like next-door's cat.
Oh, please Mum, let me
Have my own pet.
It could be a dog,
The long ones like logs.
It doesn't have to be hairy,
So it won't be all scary.
If we have one that's smooth,
I'm sure Dad would approve.
Oh, please Mum, let me
Have my own pet.
I won't mind giving it a cuddle,
If it's jumped in a puddle.
It will listen to me talk,
When I take it for a walk.
If we need to go far,
We can go in your car.
I know even the vet,
Will say it's the best pet.
Oh, please Mum, let me
Have my own pet!'

Jordan Gregory (9)
Llangeitho Primary School, Tregaron

Holiday

Happiness is like . . .

Waking every new morning
Hearing the birds singing
In the enormous tree in my garden.

Seeing my family at breakfast
Greeting me with a welcome smile
And kiss.

Going on my holidays (camping)
And putting up our tent
In a huge field.

Seeing and having a swim
In the cool blue Gower sea and sunbathing
Under the warmth of the summer sun.

Finishing the day
With a game of cricket
And a huge feast on the barbecue.

Megan Richards (8)
St Robert's Catholic Primary School, Aberkenfig

Macbeth

M enace to the world
A men, he cannot say
C hrist is disappointed
B eware, Macbeth is awake
E veryone is scared
T rees are dying
H e is not a good leader.

Liam Evans (11)
St Robert's Catholic Primary School, Aberkenfig

Happiness Is Like . . .

Seeing my beautiful blonde mother
Every morning when I wake up.
Drinking a lovely, hot, sweet cup of tea.
Seeing my fantastic, brilliant
Trampolining club get a high score.
Seeing my cute, sweet, baby sister
Run to me when I get home from school.
Seeing my best, pretty, fantastic
Friend in school.
Seeing a bright, sparkly, full moon
When you go to bed.
Having a fluffy, soft, warm pillow
To rest your head.
Seeing wrapped-up, coloured presents
Under the Christmas tree on Christmas morning.

Ffion Randall (8)
St Robert's Catholic Primary School, Aberkenfig

Happiness Is Like . . .

Good news knocking on my door,
Me sliding across the dance room floor.

Looking at the tree on Christmas morning,
Seeing the sun when the day is dawning.

Having a great meal,
Seeing a cat squeal.

Slipping on a banana skin,
Watching my football team win.

But the best thing is
Having a kiss and hug from Mum and Dad.

Gina Bertorelli (8)
St Robert's Catholic Primary School, Aberkenfig

My Terrible Brother

My brother is five and he's too much of a baby,
He's always in my way.
He makes a lot of noise and breaks my favourite toys,
I wish he'd leave me on my own to play.

My brother is five and he's too much of a nuisance,
He kicks me hard and sometimes pulls my hair
And when I shout, 'Clear off!' I'm the one who gets told off,
He gets a hug and kiss, which isn't fair.

My brother is five and he's too clumsy,
Don't you think it's time he went to bed?
I know it's still the morning, but I'm sure I saw him yawning,
I'll go and get a pillow for his head.

My brother is five but he thinks he's grown-up,
He's trying to look older but his gumboots trip him over,
He is always wearing boots which are too large
And he shouts at me and stamps when I'm in charge.

My brother is five and he's too messy,
He covers all my books with glue.
Mum says it is his age, I'd like to put him in a cage,
My terrible brother who's five!

James Jones (8)
St Robert's Catholic Primary School, Aberkenfig

Silly Hallowe'en

Ghosts and ghouls are silly fools
Silly witches are terrible snitches
Wizards stink like sticky ink
But who's hiding behind that silly mask going *moo*?
I think I'll run up to him and shout, *'Boo!'*

Holly Jade Bowen (10)
St Robert's Catholic Primary School, Aberkenfig

Being Frightened Is Like . . .

At Hallowe'en it is like seeing a ghost, a spider, a rattlesnake
And just one bite and you're dead.

Seeing a scary skeleton rise
From its old, terrifying, awful, ugly grave.

Being in the dark with bats
Gnats and redback spiders.

Lying in bed and seeing a scary shadow
Coming up the stairs.

Seeing your mum dead on the floor
With blood all over her - rosy red, dark, lumpy blood.

Being in a pitch-dark closet and you hear a noise
That is hissing, rattling, creaking and you don't know what it is.

You are in bed, you hear a bouncing sound,
A doll is bouncing the ball, so you go back to bed.
The next night you hear it again, you go to see what it is
And *roooaaahh!* You're stabbed!

Emma Chumley (8)
St Robert's Catholic Primary School, Aberkenfig

Go-Karting

When I go karting
I whiz around the track
I always get excited
And hate to be at the back
I like to go racing
I don't like to brag
But nine times out of ten
I take the chequered flag!

Oliver Marks (8)
St Robert's Catholic Primary School, Aberkenfig

My Great Day

I saw sisters, one as small as a Shetland pony
And one as tall as a Christmas tree and bright, covered presents
I saw my brother in his cool pyjamas.

I heard the phone ring like thunder
And the robotic dog barked like a mouse
I heard my mum shouting at the top of her voice.

I smelt cakes baking like lightning
I smelt chips that made me feel sick.

I thought it was magnificent
Because it was fun.

Aaron Hatch (9)
St Robert's Catholic Primary School, Aberkenfig

The First Time I Saw My Dog

I saw my dog, as small as a mouse,
And as helpless as a newborn baby.

I heard my dog barking,
Like a mouse squeaking.

I heard people chattering,
Like hyenas.

I heard cars being noisy,
Like a pack of bulls.

I thought of what we would do,
In the future.

Ryan Nolan (9)
St Robert's Catholic Primary School, Aberkenfig

My First Hallowe'en

It's a cold, dark night
I dress up to fright
With my cape and my fangs
My face painted white.

My big brother takes me by the hand
To walk down the street
We knock on the doors
I say, 'Trick or treat?'
My bag becomes full
It is pretty handy
To put all the money in
And lots of candy.

We open the door
At the end of the night
I get out of bed
To quickly put on the light!

Amy Keepings (9)
St Robert's Catholic Primary School, Aberkenfig

Clown In A Circus Show

Once I went down
To see a funny clown.

He wore very loose jeans
And he was eating baked beans.

On his hat was a fat frog
And on his shoe was a dog.

He looked a bit like these girls
Except he had big curls.

He was so funny you wouldn't believe
That when he finished, I didn't want to leave!

Cristina Ferreira (8)
St Robert's Catholic Primary School, Aberkenfig

A Fun Day With Puppies

I saw my auntie's puppies
The puppies are as small as a mouse
And they are pretty.

I saw lots and lots of puppies
Playing like cats and dogs, but not as bad
But more funny to see.

I heard dogs barking
Loudly like lions.

I heard people talking
As quiet as a mouse.

One was left alone like a bat in the dark
I went up to her and we started playing
She bit my shoes.

I picked her up, her fur was as soft as snow
She licked me and it was as cold as ice.

I felt happy
Because she is now my puppy.

Charlotte Leston (9)
St Robert's Catholic Primary School, Aberkenfig

My Hallowe'en

I saw ghosts as white as snow
I saw werewolves with blood all over their teeth
I heard vampires scraping against the doors
I heard witches cackling around the streets
I heard ghosts *wooing* all around the houses
I smelt toffee apples as sweet as honey
I smelt chocolate as if it was melting in my mouth
I smelt sweets as if they were in my mouth
I thought it was fantastic!

Holly Richards (9)
St Robert's Catholic Primary School, Aberkenfig

Eryri

I saw the mountain, it was like a sleeping giant
Snoring softly as I was looking up at it.

I saw a group of ants in the distance
Picking their way up the rough track.

I saw sleeping lakes nestled
On the side of the mountain.

I heard the wind whistling
And whipping my hair.

I heard the call
Of the bravest bird soaring overhead.

I heard the sound of the mountain train
Trying to race us up the mountain
Huffing and puffing as it went.

I could almost taste the mountain
The stones, the rocks, the sweet grass.

I smelt such beautiful heather
Growing through the grass.

I smelt the pure air
Suddenly I thought I was lucky to have a sense of smell.

I thought the café had seen better days
But a cold drink made it OK . . .

Constance Osgood-Finney (9)
St Robert's Catholic Primary School, Aberkenfig

Macbeth

M onstrous
A killer
C old-blooded
B east
E vil
T his is how he is
H orrifying.

Jonathan Russell (10)
St Robert's Catholic Primary School, Aberkenfig

Last Christmas

I saw my family laugh joyfully
As if there were seven elephants in the room
I saw the Christmas lights glittering and sparkling
As if Jesus was one of them
I saw my niece glow like gold as she saw her presents.

I heard cheerful laughter come from my family
I heard my niece bang phenomenally on my new keyboard
I heard the thanks from my family for all their presents.

I smelt the luxurious cooked dinner as I passed by
I tasted some of the most appetising chocolate
I smelt the wine fizz and splat all over the place.

I thought of all my magnificent toys
And what I'm going to do with them
I thought of people who aren't as lucky as me
And how disappointed they are
I thought of what I was going to do with all of my toys
But now it's time for bed.

Leah Roberts (9)
St Robert's Catholic Primary School, Aberkenfig

My Hallowe'en Party

I saw little devils as red as a tomato
I saw loads of people running around
Like an elephant stomping its feet
I saw people knocking on the door
As loud as a lion when it roars.

I heard loads of people saying trick or treat
So loud, the windows smashed and popped
I heard people crunching like a herd of elephants
I heard children running up and down like a panda.

I smelt loads of sweets as sticky as glue and honey together
I thought it was a good night
Because I had loads of sweets and money.

Jade Radcliffe (9)
St Robert's Catholic Primary School, Aberkenfig

My First Hallowe'en

The man dressed up as a ferocious wolf
He made me jump out of my skin.

There was a bat, he looked like he was going to kill people
With his scary fangs.

I heard lots and lots of people
Laughing like hyenas.

I heard lots and lots of horrifying music
Playing everywhere around me in every street.

I went to bed more scared than ever before
But I nearly fell out of my bed
Because I thought I saw a wolf pass my door.

I smelt my beautiful sweets
I smelt and tasted my chocolate
I tasted my apples from dunking apples.

I thought I was going to go next year
I thought I had £40 but I did not
I had a bucket full of candy.

Ffiôn Morgan (10)
St Robert's Catholic Primary School, Aberkenfig

The Hallowe'en Horror

The big bright orange pumpkin with a flickering light
Comes on in the night and gives the trick or treaters a fright.

I first hear a scream
Here comes Hallowe'en
The light goes off
And brings out the night
The coldness drifts in
And takes out the fright.

I thought hard about Hallowe'en that night
Then turned off the light!

Kristie Hore (9)
St Robert's Catholic Primary School, Aberkenfig

A Poem About Our Holiday

I felt . . .
An anaconda, long, fat, heavy
With rough skin like sandpaper,
The heavy, fast rain like a shower,
The big steering wheel like rubber,
The hard, metal, cold handles on wooden doors,
The force pushing my mouth on speed,
A wet, shiny sea lion.

I saw . . .
A big field of caravans
Like roller coaster rides,
Big, brown feathery wings on the vulture,
The yellow Pontin's sign on the black gate,
A green lizard from the faraway desert.

I smelt . . .
Chlorine from the big swimming pool,
Cows eating grass in their field,
The lovely beefburgers,
Hot custard with jelly.

I ate . . .
Hot chillies with buttery mashed potatoes,
Crunchy fish fingers that were so nice,
A juicy, soft and crunchy tuna baguette.

Jordan Young, Cameron Martin & Shane Lewis (9)
St Robert's Catholic Primary School, Aberkenfig

Macbeth

M acbeth the murderer
A nd Lady Macbeth the decisive one
C ousin King Duncan didn't expect
B etrayal from Macbeth
E vil Lady Macbeth had to deal with this
T he three witches were pleased
H e never, ever slept again.

Sirage Bellia (10)
St Robert's Catholic Primary School, Aberkenfig

My Cousin's Christening

I saw St Robert's church shining in the sun
The colours were a dull grey and a very pale, yellowy-cream
I saw the priest wearing a glazing, shimmering white vestment
It was shining in the sun
I saw my cousin's family say thank you to the priest
Because they were proud of my cousin getting Christened.

I heard my cousin crying as loud as chairs clattering on the floor
So I could then not hear what the priest was saying
I heard all the family talking as quietly as a mouse
So they could hear themselves and the priest.

I smelt the delicious food that was at the party
That was after the Christening
I touched the cold, soft hands of family members
I touched the glass of the cups that were as cold as ice
I touched the plates that were as bumpy as rocks and as warm as fur
I felt very happy for going to the Christening.

Lowrie Dean (9)
St Robert's Catholic Primary School, Aberkenfig

In August, A Surprise Party

I saw all my best friends playing like maniacs
I saw adults drinking bottles of wine in a bar
I saw lots of people lining up for a fab drink.

I heard people laughing like elephants screaming
I heard people talking as loud as a stampede of buffalo.

I smelt the sparkling wine at midnight glistening like diamonds
I tasted the delicious sausages and lovely cake that tasted sweet
I touched the fantastic balloon that floated like a bird of prey.

I had a fantastic feeling but was also very sad
Like falling off a cliff.

James Pare (9)
St Robert's Catholic Primary School, Aberkenfig

My Holiday

I was at the airport
I got on the plane and I heard a tremendous noise
As if I had just been by a cliff and had fallen off.

I got to the airport
And I saw my nan and grandad
And felt as if I had won the lottery.

We went to the town
And we tasted this drink
That made you crazy like a monkey.

And after a while we went back
I was asleep in the car like a hedgehog in its bed
And the next day I got up like a sprinter on a track.

Soon, it was time to go home
I was really sad and got on the plane as sad as a mouse
I got home and was happy to see my dog
She jumped up like a monkey
And I really enjoyed my holiday.

Bronte Marlborough (9)
St Robert's Catholic Primary School, Aberkenfig

My Cousin's Birth

I saw the nurses around my auntie
I saw my nan and uncle and family gather round her
I saw the baby coming into the world
I heard the baby crying like a herd of elephants
And it made me cry too
I heard my auntie scream like a hyena
I heard the nurses talking to her
I felt really happy for my auntie and uncle
I felt really emotional for my cousin
I felt quite upset because my auntie was in pain.

Paige Coward (9)
St Robert's Catholic Primary School, Aberkenfig

My Fourth Holiday In Spain

I saw sandy coloured villas with golden balconies
I saw shops and pubs in all bright colours
I saw lovely beaches with sparkling sea.

I heard splashing in the pool and shouting
As if they had a bell on every tooth
I heard talking when people passed
I heard music in some cars as loud as a *bang!*

I smelt chlorine in the pool, it was a bad smell
I smelt the creamy suntan lotion my mum had
I smelt Spanish food, it had a very good smell.

I thought about all of my holiday on the aeroplane
I thought about the fun things I did
I thought about going home to Wales.

Bethan John (9)
St Robert's Catholic Primary School, Aberkenfig

My Hallowe'en Holiday

I saw big, fat pumpkins
I saw little girls and boys dressed up
As little scary ghosts, witches and devils
I saw a little girl with several slithering snakes in her hair
Luckily, they were fake and not real.

I heard little people knocking as loud as thunder
I heard people saying trick or treat
Like laughing hyenas.

I smelt chocolate and sweets and toffee apples
I tasted chocolate and sticky sweets.

I thought that the snakes were fake
And what am I going to do tomorrow?
I have to wait for next year all over again.

Catalin Mellor (9)
St Robert's Catholic Primary School, Aberkenfig

Christmas Last Year

I saw my fantastic presents under my Christmas tree
I saw the decorations on the tree as if they were looking at me
I saw my mum coming down the stairs so happy
That she was as loud as a lion.

I heard my mum ripping her presents and drinking her tea
As if she was a dog digging a hole
I heard my dad knocking on the door
I heard my mum open the door and she called me.

I smelt the dinner being cooked as if a mixer was going on fast speed
I tasted the sweets that I had for Christmas
I tasted the dinner as happy as a tiger eating his meat.

I thought of what Jesus said
I thought it was time for bed
I thought I can't wait for next year
I thought that God and Jesus were near.

Isobel Rees (9)
St Robert's Catholic Primary School, Aberkenfig

The First Time I Went To A Football Match

I saw the footballers as fast as leopards
I saw a ball as round as the Earth
I saw the crowd cheering madly.

I heard the crowd cheering as loud as a herd of elephants
I heard the whack of a ball, like a brick hitting the floor
I heard sausages frying and sizzling.

I thought the scent of hot dogs smelt like chocolate
I thought the smell of Coke and beer wasn't very nice
I thought the footballers were as good as David Beckham.

Cian Watkins (9)
St Robert's Catholic Primary School, Aberkenfig

Simile Poem

A sea lion on the ice
Like a baby on the slide.
A gerbil in its cage
Like a man in a prison cell.
A penguin in the sea
Like a glider in the sky.
A tiger in the jungle
Like a hunter on a safari trail.
A bat in its sleep
Like a man abseiling a building.
A fox in its hole
Like a baby in a cot.
A snake in its skin
Like a banana in its peel.
A shark on the hunt
Like a man on the chase.

Matthew Roche (10)
St Robert's Catholic Primary School, Aberkenfig

My First Ice Hockey Game

I saw the Mighty Devils score an overhead goal
As if the puck had wings and flew into the net
I saw the fans shouting tremendously and jumping for joy
Like a kangaroo or as if they has just found gold
I saw the ice was as smooth and chilly
As the snow at the North Pole.

I heard the people cheering loudly
I heard the skates on the ice
I heard and smelt the yummy food.

I can be happy like a monkey
I can be happy like a fish.

Justyna Mikusek (10)
St Robert's Catholic Primary School, Aberkenfig

My First Day In Wildlife

I saw bright, colourful daisies
I saw a small, gentle ladybird climbing over my toe
Trying to get its way through the grass
I saw birds swoop over me.

I heard bees buzzing in my ear
I heard the grass crunching as I took my steps
I heard my mum talking beside me.

I smelt honey from the buttercups
I smelt beautiful peach from the flowers
I smelt the apples from the apple trees.

I thought I don't want this day to end
I thought the petals were so soft
I thought the ladybird was so cute.

Natasha Evans (9)
St Robert's Catholic Primary School, Aberkenfig

Time

Time is a funny thing
It never seems to end
It's almost like a trap
You'll never find the bend.

Time is good
And time is bad
Time is funny
And time is sad.

It's up to you
To make it good
I'll try
I wish you would.

Brógan Watkins (11)
St Robert's Catholic Primary School, Aberkenfig

Macbeth

M acbeth murders tonight
A cts before morning light
C riminal crime he commits
B attered into bits
E very night he dreads
T he terrible deed he committed
H e committed the crime, Lady Macbeth calls him a coward no more.

Callum Smeaton (11)
St Robert's Catholic Primary School, Aberkenfig

My Holiday In Florida With My Family

I saw all the mighty Disney characters
I saw palm trees with their leaves a beautiful green
I saw sand with a beautiful yellow colour
I saw cacti that had thorns as sharp as razors
I saw two lizards in a beautiful brown colour
I heard cars beeping their horns quickly
I heard people on the speeding roller coaster
I thought it was great and I would like to go again!

Sorcha Davies (10)
St Robert's Catholic Primary School, Aberkenfig

Macbeth

M urder by Macbeth
A men stuck in the back of his throat
C ruel Lady Macbeth persuaded Macbeth to do this
B lood that could turn an ocean red
E very day will Macbeth remember that night
T his will never be forgotten
H ell he will go.

Emily Thomas (11)
St Robert's Catholic Primary School, Aberkenfig

Macbeth

M emories of that deadly night
   still lay in the hands of Macbeth
A lone in the room with the king,
   the daggers go straight into him
C an King Duncan forgive him or when Macbeth dies,
   will King Duncan haunt him?
B lood everywhere, as the daggers
   are in the hands of the guards
E very time Macbeth looks at his hands
   he sees blood
T aunted by Duncan
   for the rest of his life
H e will not be forgiven
   and Heaven will close its gates to him.

Shannon Bargery (11)
St Robert's Catholic Primary School, Aberkenfig

The Hallowe'en Night

I saw lots of pumpkins as orange as a hot, flaming sun
I saw lots of witches with dark and pointy noses
I saw lots of vampires with pointy teeth and blood dripping down.

I heard people shouting out loudly, 'Trick or treat'
I heard the doors being knocked hollowly.

I smelt the dark air
I smelt the lovely sweets
I smelt the lovely money.

I thought I would have more money than last year
I thought I would have more sweets than last year
I thought I would have more stuff than last year.

Joseph Hapgood (9)
St Robert's Catholic Primary School, Aberkenfig

The Witches' Spell
(Inspired by 'Macbeth')

'Double, double, toil and trouble
Fire burn and cauldron bubble'.

Eye of lady
And toe of dog
Fur of cat
And tongue of frog.

Spider's legs
And tail of an ogre
Shiny stars
And mammoth's shoulder.

Eye of dragon
And toe of tortoise
Lion's mane
And nail of porpoise.

'For a charm
Of powerful trouble
Like a hell-broth
Boil and bubble.

Double, double, toil and trouble
Fire burn and cauldron bubble'.

Lydia Price (10)
St Robert's Catholic Primary School, Aberkenfig

Macbeth

M acbeth had killed the king
A nd terror in the castle
C ruel Macbeth could do such a thing
B ecause of Lady Macbeth's cruelty
E vil Lady Macbeth who told Macbeth to do such a thing
T here will be no more sleep
H e has murdered sleep.

Emma Dodd (10)
St Robert's Catholic Primary School, Aberkenfig

The Witches' Spell
(Inspired by 'Macbeth')

*'Double, double, toil and trouble
Fire burn and cauldron bubble'.*

Silver moon
Crystal star
Locked up
In a big, dark jar.

Eye of newt
Ear of ogre
Tongue of dog
Leg of frog.

Shoe of horse
Tail of rat
Buzzing fly
And crazy cat.

Mixed up with
A big sharp charm
Mix it up with
A fat ape's arm.

*'Double, double, toil and trouble
Fire burn and cauldron bubble'.*

Jessica Buller (10)
St Robert's Catholic Primary School, Aberkenfig

Bananas

B ruised bananas never eat
A nd green bananas are too sweet
N ice bananas are the ones you want
A nd pink bananas are semicircles and neat, but
N ever eat them because they taste like feet
A ll bananas have different tastes and sizes
S ome of them, be careful, they may hold a nasty surprise.

Emilie James (10)
St Robert's Catholic Primary School, Aberkenfig

Macbeth

M acbeth does murder Duncan
A nd the guards are blamed
C ruel Lady Macbeth does not care, she wants Duncan dead
and her husband king
B loody Duncan lies dead in his bed
E veryone is shocked
T he ghost of Duncan will forever haunt Macbeth
H e goes to pieces.

Taija Pengilly (11)
St Robert's Catholic Primary School, Aberkenfig

The Sea

Beneath the waves and the crashing tide
Nobody knows what its depths hide.

Mystical creatures nobody knows
New species of fish is what the scientists suppose.

Lost civilisations, treasure and gold
Maybe one day, the story will unfold.

Laura Shillibier (10)
St Robert's Catholic Primary School, Aberkenfig

Boo!

Ghostly, ghastly, scary ghouls
What happens when they go, *boo!*
Ghostly, ghastly, scary ghouls
I really wonder when they go, *boo!*
Ghostly, ghastly, scary ghouls
What will happen when I go, *boo!*
Ghostly, ghastly, scary ghouls
Do they really just go, *boo!*

Jack Evans (10)
St Robert's Catholic Primary School, Aberkenfig

Macbeth

M acbeth has killed the king
A horrible deed and a horrible cousin
C ruel cousin he is
B lood-stained hands
E ven when the children were praying, amen was stuck in his throat
T he murderer is Macbeth
H e will sleep no more.

Jordan Hatch (11)
St Robert's Catholic Primary School, Aberkenfig

Simile Poem

The monkey is in its banana tree
Like a human on a diving board.
The chick is in its egg
Like a seed in a watermelon.
The rabbit is in its hole
Like a child under his bed.
The cheetah is in its desert
Like a car on the motorway.
The frog is in its pond
Like lava in a volcano.

Peter Devonshire (11)
St Robert's Catholic Primary School, Aberkenfig

Macbeth

M urder
A nd a
C owardly Macbeth killed his king
B rutally he did it too
E vening night the king died
T he bloody stained dagger
H e pierced through his heart.

Ethan Marlborough (10)
St Robert's Catholic Primary School, Aberkenfig

Witches' Spell
(Inspired by 'Macbeth')

*'Double, double, toil and trouble
Fire burn and cauldron bubble'.*

Head of fish and eye of dog
Blind man's tongue and leg of frog

Hair of man and fin of whale
Toe of cat and snowstorm's hail

Witch's laugh and wizard's lungs
Children's teeth and slimy bugs

Eye of newt and blood of rat
Ear of rabbit and wing of bat.

*'Double, double, toil and trouble
Fire burn and cauldron bubble'.*

Michael Thomas (10)
St Robert's Catholic Primary School, Aberkenfig

Simile Poem

The eagle soars through the sky
Like a bullet coming out of a gun.

The ant is in his anthill
Like a square of chocolate in a king-sized bar.

A bat is hanging in its cave
Like a pendulum on a clock.

The salmon is climbing up his stream
Like a football being booted up a pitch.

The dog is in his street
Like a lolly in the freezer.

Sean Cooke (10)
St Robert's Catholic Primary School, Aberkenfig

Witches' Spell
(Inspired by 'Macbeth')

'Double, double, toil and trouble
Fire burn and cauldron bubble'.

A little bit of posh
A bit of squash
A bit of a boy called Josh
Who does not wash
Teacher's laugh
And half a bath
Children's teeth
And a bit of a slimy heath

'Double, double, toil and trouble
Fire burn and cauldron bubble'.

Joshua Sage (11)
St Robert's Catholic Primary School, Aberkenfig

Simile Poem

The bird is in its nest
Like a baby in its crib.

The shark is in the sea
Like a person in a swimming pool.

A giraffe is eating leaves
Like someone eating salad.

The bull is in its charge
Like a football going into a net.

The pig is in the mud
Like a person in the bath.

Joshua Paget-Howe (10)
St Robert's Catholic Primary School, Aberkenfig

Christmas

C hristmas time is here once more
H appy children, toys galore
R udolph's nose is shining red
I cicles hanging from the window ledge
S tars are shining brightly above
T he time is here that all children love
M erry songs sung by everyone
A nd all the cooking has been done
S inging and dancing around the Christmas tree

I wonder if Father Christmas will leave any presents for me
S tockings hanging from the end of my bed

H ooray, it's Christmas time
E ven though I'm only nine
R inging bells and Christmas food
E verybody's in a good mood, because . . .

Christmas is here!

Rosie Plimmer (9)
Swiss Valley Primary School, Llanelli

My Family

My family may not be big
But it means so much to me
My mum, my aunt, my pets
Are the best that there could be.

I love the time we have
When we go out for the day
To castles, museums, or shops
Or to the park to play.

So size doesn't matter
On how big a family should be
I know that I love them
And they love me.

Ryan Samuel Davies (9)
Swiss Valley Primary School, Llanelli

Woodland

In the woodland there are monkeys
In the woodland there are wasps
People being stung
There are acorns on the trees
What attacks all the squirrels
Who store the nuts for the winter
And wake up early in spring?
Making trouble everywhere
Throwing nuts everywhere
'I can't stand it!'
The trees are blowing
With the leaves everywhere
Big brown bears shouting, *'Roar!'*
Making noises everywhere
'I'm out of there!'

Rhydian Glyn Ken Jones (9)
Swiss Valley Primary School, Llanelli

My Dog

My dog is mad
My dog is crazy
And her name is Honey
If you see her
Don't go near her
You might catch
Her craziness
If you want to talk
To my dog
Just give us a ring
And we'll put Honey on
But just to warn you
She barks pretty loud!

Amy Elise May Williams (9)
Swiss Valley Primary School, Llanelli

A Poem About My Family

Lucy (me)
My name is Lucy,
Yes, that's me,
I once got stung by a bumblebee.

Ben
My little brother is Ben,
When his friends come over,
They like to make a den.

Rachel
My sister is called Rachel,
She is sixteen
And she likes to wear green.

Thomas
Thomas is my older brother,
He likes to play rugby,
I love him still, even though he bugs me.

Mammy
I love my mammy,
She always takes me to Tammy,
She is better than a nanny.

Daddy
I love my daddy,
He is the best,
Better than the rest.

Lucy Cara Havard (9)
Swiss Valley Primary School, Llanelli

The Zoo

When you take a trip to the zoo,
There are so many things to see,
Elephants, monkeys and white tigers
And maybe a bumblebee.

Giraffes so tall and lions proud,
Both can be seen in their lair,
Fishes that swim in the water
And round the corner, a polar bear.

Monkeys, gorillas and chimpanzees,
Are all types of apes
And the foods they feast on,
Include apples, bananas and grapes.

The aquarium is very entertaining,
There are fish of every kind,
Plus, in the outdoor pool,
Dolphins and seals you might find.

Now, don't forget the twilight zone,
With bats, oh so blind,
They use their sensors to get around,
Their friends, how do they find?

But what if they would rather be free?
Where would they rather be born?
I wouldn't like to be held there,
I don't think it's very fair,
But I still enjoy the zoo.

Kamran Raza (9)
Swiss Valley Primary School, Llanelli

Hallowe'en Night

It's Hallowe'en night
Oh, what a fright
I hope I don't get scared tonight
When the sun goes out.

Come out if you dare
Or the witches and wizards
Will give you a scare
Beware!
Prepare for a scare!

Hallowe'en is at its peak
Villains are out
Tonight
At midnight.

Tonight
That is when
The villains' powers
Are strongest!

Lyndsey Morris (9)
Swiss Valley Primary School, Llanelli

Football Rocks!

I love watching football,
Celtic are my team,
They play their football at Parkhead,
The best I've ever seen.

I love watching football,
Especially when we score,
Jan Vennegoor of Hesselink,
He's scoring more and more!

I love watching football,
I go there with my dad,
We have a Bovril at half-time,
We both are Celtic mad!

Conor Polson (9)
Swiss Valley Primary School, Llanelli

My Holiday In Scotland

Everything was quiet on the farm,
The only sound I could hear at night was the frogs croaking,
The chimney stack was quietly smoking;
In the distance I could see sheep, they looked like little cotton balls
And the fields were divided by drystone walls;
The farmer was busy doing his daily chores,
Dressed in his wellies and his old tatty clothes;
The field was ploughed, the animals were fed
And the pigs were sent to market;
At the end of the day, the tractor came up the lane,
The farmer drove into the yard where he parked it;
The farmer's wife was jolly and fun, she taught us rhymes
And this is one -
'A wee, wee man with a red, red coat,
A staff in his hand
And a stone in his throat.'
It sometimes rained, but the air was clean
And we didn't want to come home from where we'd just been.

Amelia Thomas (9)
Swiss Valley Primary School, Llanelli

Sunday Night

Running all around
Looking for my things
My ruler, my pencil, my head.

Where are my socks?
Where are my shoes?
My coat, my shirt in red?

School is tomorrow
It's Sunday night
I'm exhausted
Where is my bed?

Bethan Harriet Jones (9)
Swiss Valley Primary School, Llanelli

My Pet Dog, Sophie

My dog, Sophie, is my pet,
She doesn't like to see the vet,
I like to take her to the park,
Where she runs around and gives a bark.

She likes to eat lots of food,
I never see her in a bad mood,
She likes to chew my father's shoe
And my mother's slippers too.

Sophie likes to play with toys,
Her squeaky ball makes a noise,
I like to give her lots of treats,
Her favourite treats are doggy sweets.

Sophie is a real cutie,
Black and white, oh, what a beauty!
Soft and fluffy and really smart,
I love Sophie with all my heart!

Caitlin Lauren Evans (9)
Swiss Valley Primary School, Llanelli

Christmas

Have you heard the sleigh bells ring in the night?
Have you heard the reindeer hooves on your roof at night?
Have you seen a snowman walk up the garden path?
Have you seen Santa putting toys on your hearth?

I've heard the sleigh bells ring in the night
I'm sure I've heard reindeer hooves in the middle of the night
But I've never seen a snowman walk up our garden path
And I've never seen Santa putting toys on our hearth.

Maybe I will this year
Merry Christmas!

Zoe Alexandra Austin (9)
Swiss Valley Primary School, Llanelli

My Day

Today is my day,
Is it yours too?
If it is, then enjoy it
I'll make you laugh so much
That . . .
You'll cry
And when you've stopped
It will be time for lunch
Then after lunch
We'll play a game of footie
We'll score goals against the boys
(Because they're the worst)
Anyway, let's just walk
Hand in hand
That's my day.

Shauna Davies (9)
Swiss Valley Primary School, Llanelli

There Was A Man Called . . .

There was a man called Dan
And he drives a mini van
His favourite rock star
Lives really far
And that's all about the man called Dan.

There was a man called Josh
And he had a really bad cough
We do not know why he had a bad cough
But we feel really sorry for that man called Josh.

There was a man called Dominic
But we don't know why he was so sick
I think someone gave him a kick
So that's why I think that the man called Dominic felt so sick.

Rehaan Ahktaar (9)
Swiss Valley Primary School, Llanelli

The Acrostic Poem About James Bond

J ames Bond is a secret agent
A uric Goldfinger is the world's greatest gold smuggler
M is the head of MI5 in the James Bond films
E ngland is where MI5 headquarters are
S peeding in fast cars is what he loves to do

B ond is the best, going round with his Walther PPK
O ther agents are not like him
N obody does it better than Bond
'D ie Another Day' was a James Bond film

G oldfinger loves gold
O ddjob is his assistant
L oves golden guns
D ead is what he want James Bond to be
F ighting James Bond he loves to do
I nside he is dangerous and he is SPECTRE
N ever gives up until 007 kills him
G oldfinger has no longer got an assistant, Oddjob is dead
E is the end, but he'll always be back
R emember me, I'm James Bond, 007.

Michael Robert Fry (9)
Swiss Valley Primary School, Llanelli

Hamsters - My Poem

Hamsters are small that chew blocks of wood
They're cute, cuddly little things
Being what hamsters should
Sometimes they might chew your sweater
But when they're sad, you make them feel better
They run around in their ball
And to them, you are quite tall
They run in their tunnels, they run around
They don't even make a sound
Apart from their tiny squeak.

Hamsters are black, hamsters are brown
They're the colours of the town
Which is sweet, gentle and kind
A hamster is a child's very best friend
You're true friendship shall never end
As long as you shall live.

This shows how much my pet hamster means to me!

Kirsty Leigh Thomas (9)
Swiss Valley Primary School, Llanelli

My Bike

For Christmas I had a new bike
It had a lovely big seat
On the wheel, it said Nike
It's a present you can't beat

I ride it on the street
I go fast, fast, fast
My friends I always beat
I never come last, last, last

My safety gear I always wear
When I ride my bike
Because you have to take care
Doing things you like

When the day is over
I put my bike away
In the garage with Daddy's Rover
Until another day.

Bethany Davies (9)
Swiss Valley Primary School, Llanelli

Friendship

F is for friendship that I give to others
R is for relationships that I share with my friends
I is for I love you
E is for enjoying being a friend
N is for Nanny and Bampie who will always be there
D is for Dan, a good friend of mine
S is for spoiling when I see Nan and Dad
H is for hello that I say to people I meet
I is for independence as I grow up
P is for perfect, that everyone is.

Chirelle Morris (8)
Talgarth Primary School, Brecon

I Wish . . .

I wish I were a fire-breathing dragon
Slowly moving on legs
Scales red like blood
As hard as rock
Battling other dragons
With wings as big as a cave

I wish I were I fire-breathing dragon
With huge jaw muscles
And razor-sharp teeth
Beady eyes
The size of someone's face

I wish I were a fire-breathing dragon
With a huge nose
A scar on my face
Big claws, black as midnight
As sharp as a knife.

Ben Peters (7)
Talgarth Primary School, Brecon

The Environment

E is for ecology which is what we should all know
N is for Native Indians scratching in the earth
V is for voles digging everywhere
I is for interest in how we are helping
R is for rocks millions of years old
O is for oxygen that keeps nature alive
N is for nature that lives all around us
M is for magma erupting from volcanoes
E is for enemies of nature we are
N is for *no pollution*
T is for trees, plants and wildlife.

Brynley Eckley (8)
Talgarth Primary School, Brecon

The Environment

I love the environment
The trees swaying in the wind
Giving us oxygen
The grass that grows tall
So that you can play hide-and-seek in it
The ponds, rivers and seas with reeds growing on the bank
The river flowing slowly then getting faster as it reaches the sea
The animals that play with you
Creatures crawling all over you
But most of all, I love the environment because
There are animals, creatures and living things
Land and earth
All the things that make the environment
That God made for us to enjoy, love and look after.

Millie Jones (8)
Talgarth Primary School, Brecon

I Wish . . .

I wish I were a bird
Flying through the sky
People looking small
Like tiny circles
Rushing around

I wish I were a dolphin
Jumping up from the ocean
Diving back and seeing
Fish passing by
Under the water
Gold treasure from a ship

I wish I were a pony
Smelling the fresh green grass
That grows in the fields
Getting groomed ready for the competition.

Cellan Davies & Charmaine Carey (7)
Talgarth Primary School, Brecon

I Wish . . .

I wish I could run so fast
I would run like the wind and not stop
Until I ran out of breath
I would run so fast
I could win a race, beat everyone
And shout out loud
'I've won!'

I wish I were a famous footballer
I would score lots of goals
From the halfway line with my golden boot
A fantastic pass to my teammate
Free kicks and corners
Scoring from outside my own box.

I wish I were a famous footballer
I would run like the wind
Not get tackled
Sneak a shot in the net
It would swoop like a bird into the top corner
Past the keeper
Goal!

Ceri Jones (7)
Talgarth Primary School, Brecon

Love

Love is red like a strawberry
It tastes like a red juicy apple
Love feels like a kiss from your mum
It smells like fresh flowers growing in the garden
Love reminds me of when I see my dad.

Ethan Hatton (7)
Talgarth Primary School, Brecon

I Wish . . .

I wish I were a fish
That swam everywhere
Darting from place to place
A swordfish swimming through the ocean
With his sharp nose
Cutting through the water

I wish I were a rabbit
Bouncing up and down
Through the green grass
In the wild fields
Moving faster
Hiding from the enemies
Big beady eyes

I wish I were a cat
Catching mice
Pouncing from the bushes
Catching its prey
Purring when it's happy.

Jack Carey & Morgan Skyrme (8)
Talgarth Primary School, Brecon

Anger

Anger sounds like a loud rocket going into space
Anger tastes like jam too sweet in my mouth
Anger is as black as the night-time
Anger smells like wood smoke
Anger feels hard like a rock
Anger reminds me of fighting with my brother.

Corey Thompson (8)
Talgarth Primary School, Brecon

The Environment

T is for textures all around us
H is for harvest time when we thank God
E is for everything that God has given us

E is for environment, the trees and grass
N is for nettles slowly swaying in the wind
V is for views of the Brecon Beacons so high in the sky
I is for information on keeping it clean and tidy
R is for rabbits hopping around my feet
O is for the oxygen that trees give to us
N is for nests with birds all snug inside
M is for mulch that feeds the soil
E is for Earth that we are living on
N is for never throw your litter on the ground
T is for Talgarth, my hometown.

Caitlin Pugh & Megan Jones (8)
Talgarth Primary School, Brecon

The Seasons

T is for trees growing in the spring with buds on the branches
H is for harvest, gathering vegetables and storing them safe
E is for the environment spread over the world

S is for summer when the sun shines as bright as a fire
E is for the earth providing all the food we need
A is for apples, sweet and juicy on the tree
S is for snow that falls in the winter
O is for oranges that grow in the summer
N is for nights that get longer in autumn
S is for spring, watching lambs jump and flowers in the garden starting to push through.

Imaani Thomas & Kate Jones (8)
Talgarth Primary School, Brecon

The Environment

T is for trees that give you oxygen
H is for harvest with vegetables to eat
E is for the environment to keep tidy

E is for eggs that hatch when it's warm
N is for neat and tidy gardens to care for
V is for views of the world we see in photos
I is for information to keep tidy
R is for rhinos that are black and rare
O is for oranges that grow on trees
N is for naughty girls and boys that make a mess
M is for moles digging underground
E is for elephants that are killed for their tusks
N is for never make a mess because nature is important
T is for tidy, keep everything tidy!

Georgia Tinton (8)
Talgarth Primary School, Brecon

I Wish . . .

I wish I were a superhero
Flying round and round
Faster and faster, saving the world

I wish I were a superhero
Climbing up buildings
Swinging from house to house
Faster and faster, saving the world

I wish I were a superhero
Throwing far and fast
Destroying the enemy
Faster and faster, saving the world!

Kieran Jones (7)
Talgarth Primary School, Brecon

The Seasons

S is for the sea, rough but sometimes calm in summertime
E is for eggs just being laid by chickens in spring
A is for apples landing on my head as they fall off the trees
S is for something special that might happen through the year
O is for oh thank you for everything we have, like apples and grapes
N is for night-time, so black in the winter
S is for seeing the Brecon Beacons in wintertime all covered in snow.

Ross Leighton (8)
Talgarth Primary School, Brecon

Meg, My Sheepdog

Meg was my sheepdog,
She was black and white,
Like the keys of a piano,
Meg had a white ring around her belly,
Like a rubber ring,
But best of all,
Meg loved playing football.

Ben Harvey (7)
Ysgol Cilcennin, Lampeter

Blue

Blue is the sky,
Blue is the bit in your eye,
Blue is like mist in the morning,
Blue is a blue flower,
Blue is one of the colour in the rainbow,
Blue is the colour of my nose in the cold,
Blue is the water of the world,
Blue is my favourite colour.

Benito Thomas Gilmore (10)
Ysgol Cilcennin, Lampeter

Shooting Stars

Shooting stars are yellow and bright,
Flying high in the deep, dark night.

Watching shooting stars, here and there,
Shooting stars are moving brightly everywhere.

I hope I might just see a shooting star tonight,
In the deep, dark night.

Natasha Pearce (8)
Ysgol Cilcennin, Lampeter

Animals

Some animals are smelly like jelly
Some are small like a ping-pong ball
Or as tall like a grand hall.

Water animals can scare a fly
Oh why, oh why, do animals fly?
Like an eagle in the sky
Oh why, oh why, oh why?

Dale Robert Firth (8)
Ysgol Cilcennin, Lampeter

My Dog, Kissi

My dog's name is Kissi,
She can be very silly.

Kissi has a set of teeth, which she likes to use,
She chews, chews and chews!

Kissi loves to bark
At her own reflection,
Which proves just how silly Kissi can be.

Crystal Gina Gilmore (10)
Ysgol Cilcennin, Lampeter

Dogs

I like animals,
But my favourite animals are . . .
Dogs!
I've got so many of them,
I don't know who's who!
I've got black ones and brown ones,
I've got long ones and tall ones,
I've got fat ones and thin ones,
I've got spotty ones and striped ones,
I've got fluffy ones and smooth ones,
I've got rough ones and soft ones!
Now you know everything about me and my dogs,
So you now know what my favourite animal is.

Sioned Jones (8)
Ysgol Cilcennin, Lampeter

Green

Green is the grass,
Which grows in the field.

Green is the camouflage,
Of my army trousers.

Green is the moss,
Which clings to the bark of a dead tree.

Green is the leaves,
Which grow on the trees in spring and summertime.

Chameleons can be green,
When they are in front of green leaves.

Green is one of my favourite colours,
It reminds me of the start of springtime.

Nathaniel Sawyer (8)
Ysgol Cilcennin, Lampeter

The Sky

The sky is so high,
Like a flying butterfly.

Why is the sky so high?
Maybe so that all the birds and aeroplanes can fly.

The sky is so blue,
Like a blue, blue lagoon.

Why is the sky so blue?
Maybe so everyone can see the clouds in the sky.

I like the sky when it is red and orange,
In the middle of a beautiful sunset.

Kimberley Reeves (7)
Ysgol Cilcennin, Lampeter

Dinosaurs

Dinosaurs can be as small
As a cat.
Dinosaurs can be as tall
As my house.
Dinosaurs can be wider
Than a really huge elephant.
Dinosaurs can be thinner
Than a leopard.
Dinosaurs can be as scary
As a 30 foot spider.
But best of all, I like dinosaurs
Because they're *massive!*

Ben Smithers (10)
Ysgol Cilcennin, Lampeter

My Kitten, Snuggles

My kitten is as black as the night
Her name is Snuggles because she likes lots of cuddles
She likes to sleep in the sun and roll on her tum
She is very sweet like a well-loved teddy.

She miaows and miaows
When she wants some fuss
Sometimes she can be very, very bad
But I love her and love her so much
I forget about her being naughty.

Chloe Jones (9)
Ysgol Cilcennin, Lampeter

The Party

I am waiting patiently for my friends,
At the front gate.
Munching some biscuits,
From a party plate.
Then they arrive, happy and excited,
We play in my field,
Until I am tired.

George Reynolds (7)
Ysgol Dyffryn Trannon, Trefeglwys

The Party

Parties at Christmas are the ones I like best,
With lots of music, laughter and shouting.
There will be fizzy drinks and lots of food
And sweaty people on the dance floor.

Josh Cotton (8)
Ysgol Dyffryn Trannon, Trefeglwys

The Party

For my birthday, I am having a picnic,
Five friends have come along.
We are sitting in a lovely field
And we are going to sing a song.

Hermia Hayward (7)
Ysgol Dyffryn Trannon, Trefeglwys

The Party

Sandwiches
Sandwiches
Crisps
And
More
Ice cream
Ice cream
Jelly
Galore!

Jake Tranter (8)
Ysgol Dyffryn Trannon, Trefeglwys

The Party

My birthday party
I am so excited
My friends have arrived
The party has started.

Rebecca Cotton (7)
Ysgol Dyffryn Trannon, Trefeglwys

The Game

Flying feet
Open ground
To the goal
Ball kicking
Fast running
Loads of goals
Crowd shouting.

Zoé Jones (9)
Ysgol Dyffryn Trannon, Trefeglwys

The Party

I had a party at my house,
I had a cake, it was big and round,
I had a big present,
I wonder what it is?
I try and try to think what it is,
It's a . . . ?
What a fun party!

Mia Maeér-Butterworth (7)
Ysgol Dyffryn Trannon, Trefeglwys

The Game

R unning down the pitch
U nbelievable speed
G oing to score
B eginning to sweat
Y es, he scored!

Elisabeth Owen (10)
Ysgol Dyffryn Trannon, Trefeglwys

The Game

The morning has arrived,
We're revving to go,
We jump into the car
And are zooming to the groove.

We finally get to the stadium,
Everyone is shouting,
We can hear and smell
The burgers sizzling.

We feel as good as good could be,
The men on the field shout,
'Pass the ball back to me!'
The ball passes back and forward
We scored a goal!

We see the men
With their painted faces
And hear people screaming,
We shout out loud,
'Hooray! Hooray!'

We shift on home,
For dinner and bed,
We won the game!

Kira Maeér-Butterworth (10)
Ysgol Dyffryn Trannon, Trefeglwys

The Game

N etball is my favourite game
E veryone playing and having fun
T rying to score a goal
B eating the other team
A ll of the people trying to score a goal
L eaping into the air
L aughing, yes, a goal!

Jasmine Evans (9)
Ysgol Dyffryn Trannon, Trefeglwys

The Party

Today I'm really happy,
I hope you are too,
Because it is my birthday,
Come to my party, why don't you?

Red balloons, yellow balloons,
Maybe blue or green,
Party games and party food,
What shall I have to eat?

Crisps, sandwiches and jelly are the best,
The music is loud,
The laughing is cheerful,
But now I have to go to bed
And so do you!

Rachel Mills (9)
Ysgol Dyffryn Trannon, Trefeglwys

The Party

Today is the day the party's on,
Everybody will be here, not too long,
There will be a lot of food,
I can't wait for my friend, he's a real cool dude!

The music is loud,
There will be a big, big crowd,
I can see the presents all around,
But the kitchen is out of bounds.

The people dancing are really mad,
And their socks are smelling very bad!
I love parties, it's a shame it has to end,
I think I will have another next weekend!

Tyler Thomas (8)
Ysgol Dyffryn Trannon, Trefeglwys

Rugby Is The Sport Of Wales

R ugby is the sport of Wales
U p and under, here we go
G reat players like Stephen Jones
B roken bones everywhere
Y ou really couldn't miss it for the world!

Edward Rhys Jones (11)
Ysgol Dyffryn Trannon, Trefeglwys

The Party

I got up in the morning
What did I see?
Sandwiches, jelly, jam
Chocolates and crisps
Also presents and drinks
And of course, the birthday cake!
There was music as well
Then the doorbell rang
My friends came
Carrying loads of presents
What a brilliant birthday I had
What a lucky, lucky boy I am!

Daniel Regan (9)
Ysgol Dyffryn Trannon, Trefeglwys

Snakes

S nakes slither on the jungle floor
N ever stop hunting
A ttack silently
K illing prey
E ating food
S lithering away!

Callum Shaw (9)
Ysgol Glannau Gwaun, Fishguard

The Butterfly

I did not know what I was to be
Covered in fuzz, it was hard to see
Now a butterfly, what a beautiful sight
On silken wings I take to flight

Over the hills and fields I fly
Gazing at the beautiful flowers I pass by
Now I've found a buddleia tree
Oh, what a lovely treat for tea

Under the leaves I find a space
Where I cuddle down and hide my face
The moon and stars fill the sky
Now it is time to say goodbye!

Amy Jones (9)
Ysgol Glannau Gwaun, Fishguard

Glorious Football

Football is my favourite sport,
St Mary's field is where I'm taught,
We play every Saturday, home and away,
When we score, hooray, hooray!

Chelsea are my favourite team,
Jose Mourinho keeps them keen,
Drogba, Lampard, Terry and Cole,
I shout like made when they score a goal!

I play midfield, seven on my shirt,
It's a tough old game, you may get hurt,
All the supporters shout and cheer,
Exactly what we like to hear!

Adam Charles Lewis (8)
Ysgol Glannau Gwaun, Fishguard

Football Crazy

I like playing football
When I score a goal
I'm on a roll
When I start scoring
The crowd starts roaring
Then I celebrate
Because I feel great!

Rowan Fawcett (8)
Ysgol Glannau Gwaun, Fishguard

Sharks

S harks swimming in the deep
H ave sharp teeth
A ttack in a sweep
R aging around, splashing their jaws full of prey
K illing prey for meat
S wimming away with a tummy ache.

Rhys Shaw (7)
Ysgol Glannau Gwaun, Fishguard

Pussycat

Pussycat, pussycat, up in the tree
Always counting from one to three
Pussycat, pussycat, up in the tree
Why won't you come down and have tea with me?
Now she's counting from one to ten
And now she's chasing all my hens
And that's how the story always ends!

Kai Finley Spike Williams (8)
Ysgol Glannau Gwaun, Fishguard

The Game

The whistle blows, away they go
The ball was kicked
The game was on
The players race
They push and shove
Quick tackle and then some fall
Shh! Shh! A goal is scored
We jump about
Yippee! Yippee!
The game plays on
More goals are scored
Then the whistle blows
The goals are scored
Then the whistle blows
The goals are scored
Then the whistle blows
The score's four-all
The Reds and Blues
Have made a draw.

Kevin MacDonald (8)
Ysgol Glannau Gwaun, Fishguard

I Like Rugby

I like rugby,
Rugby's my game,
Rugby's my sport,
I support Wales,
I support Scarlets,
I play for Fishguard and Goodwick,
I like scoring all the time,
I like watching rugby all the time,
I like playing rugby all the time.

Daniel Rhys Evans (9)
Ysgol Glannau Gwaun, Fishguard

Hallowe'en

The night was scary,
The night was dark,
There were witches looking eerie,
Which made the dogs bark.

After carving the pumpkins,
To make them look scary,
The children passed the window,
Looking very weary.

The children were ghosts,
Wearing white sheets,
Carrying their big bags,
Hoping for lots of treats.

The clock was ticking,
It was half-past eight,
Their mothers were hoping,
That they wouldn't be late.

Luke Richard Parr (9)
Ysgol Glannau Gwaun, Fishguard

Scooby And Shaggy

Scooby and Shaggy are scared of ghosts
They travel around in the Mystery Machine
Daphne and Fred solve all the mysteries
Velma works out who's the ghost
Scooby eats lots of Scooby snacks
And he sniffs out the ghost's tracks
The gang catch the ghost
And Scooby gets praised the most.

Zoe Mary Hayes (7)
Ysgol Glannau Gwaun, Fishguard

My Brother

My brother is weird,
He wiggles like a snake,
Giggles like a hyena,
Eats like a turtle
And is trying to grow a beard.

My brother is crazy,
He walks like a penguin,
Talks like Darth Vader,
Acts like a chicken
And his favourite thing is a daisy.

My brother is silly,
He talks in silly voices
And he does silly things,
But he is my only brother
And I do love him really.

Isobel Vickers (7)
Ysgol Glannau Gwaun, Fishguard

Fireworks

F lashing in the sky at night
I s that a rocket out of sight?
R ed, yellow, pink and blue
E very colour of the rainbow
W hirling round and round
O h, what's that squealing sound?
R oman candles and Catherine wheels
K eep well back from fireworks
S afety always comes first.

Sophie Jamieson (9)
Ysgol Glannau Gwaun, Fishguard

My Cat, Sooty

My cat, Sooty, is black and white,
Her eyes glow in the dark,
Sometimes, they give me a fright,
She's fluffy and cuddly,
But 16 years old,
The way she jumps through trees,
You would never know,
She's there in the morning,
But never at night,
She licks me and cuddles me,
Sometimes she bites,
I love my cat, Sooty,
She loves me too!

Nia Tyrrell (9)
Ysgol Glannau Gwaun, Fishguard

A Fun Day

Hooray!
It's a nice day
We're off to ride my scrambler
Up, down, around the bends
Over the jumps, my fun never ends
Unless a rain cloud should appear
Then I won't be able to steer
Dad will put my bike away
I'll come back another day.

Michael Watson (8)
Ysgol Glannau Gwaun, Fishguard

My Cat

My cat is called Tufty, he is black and fat
He's got green eyes and he sleeps on our green mat.
He chases mice in the field all through the night
But he likes to come in as soon as it's daylight.
He doesn't like to climb in the trees
Because he once got stuck and was miaowing, 'Get me down, please!'
His favourite foods are prawns and cream
And when he's eating them, he thinks he's in Heaven
                                        or having a dream.
He is my best friend and his best friend is me
We do everything together, he is a big part of my family.

Molly-May Hughes (8)
Ysgol Glannau Gwaun, Fishguard

Tommy The Shark

My name is Tommy, the fiercest shark in the sea
I live on my own and enjoy my own company
I like to scare the sea creatures and eat all the fish
The prettiest ones make a tastier dish
I hide behind the seaweed and wait for them to go past
Then I jump out and grab them - I've got them at last
I gobble them down, but my belly groans
I gurgle and burp, then I spit out the bones
I swim home happily, pleased with the day's catch
I'll return tomorrow for a new batch!

Thomas O'Sullivan (8)
Ysgol Glannau Gwaun, Fishguard

The Spider

My mum has got a spider,
Who lives in her bag of pegs,
He's big, fat and hairy,
With eight long, furry legs.

He often spins a silky web,
All around the box, then lies
In wait, sometimes for hours,
To catch those juicy flies.

Zara Thomas (9)
Ysgol Glannau Gwaun, Fishguard

Maisy, My Little Puppy

Maisy is my little puppy, as cute as can be
She is black and white, with a little bit of brown
Every day I love to play
She is such a fast runner
I know that for sure
Because she is faster than me
I love to cuddle her tight
So she never runs away at night
Maisy is the best dog ever!

Abigail Hruzik (9)
Ysgol Glannau Gwaun, Fishguard

A Christmas Wish

Father Christmas, Tinkerbell
I made a wish in the wishing well
For all the children not as lucky as me
To have hope and love and Christmas glee.

Rhiannon Warren-Hopkin (7)
Ysgol Gymraeg Bro Ogwr, Bridgend

My Uncle

My uncle is the strangest chap,
Who watches lots of telly,
His head is bald, his belly round
And his feet are rather smelly.

When I go to visit him,
He's always very pleased,
I'm sure he thinks I was born,
Purely to be teased.

He laughs at all my jokes
And lets me play his games
But if I beat him all the time
He sometimes calls me names.

I call him Uncle Craigie
When I want to buy a toy
But if he doesn't buy it
I say, 'Thanks a bunch, fat boy!'

But on the whole I like him,
He's really quite a laugh,
I would change him for the world,
Wouldn't I? Not half!

Jac Talbot (7)
Ysgol Gymraeg Bro Ogwr, Bridgend

The Cat

The cat has a furry tail
And he is friendly too
He has a warm coat of fur
And he likes to miaow and purr
He has four lovely white paws
And when he is angry
He shows his claws.

Lucy Jane Crocker (7)
Ysgol Gymraeg Bro Ogwr, Bridgend

Princess

P retty in pink is this little girl
R oses and daisies on every curl
I nsects and spiders, *argh!* she would scream
N ice things like bunnies and puppies she dreams
C rowns and jewels all over her clothes
E verything sparkles and glitters and glows
S ugar and sprinkles and everything sweet
S pecial little princess from her head to her feet.

Alyssa Davies (7)
Ysgol Gymraeg Bro Ogwr, Bridgend

My Grandad

My grandad Jack is a funny old chap
He shouts, 'Stop kicking that ball against that wall
And come sit on my knee and hear me sing like Pavarotti
Before we have our tea!'

Phoebe Ann Lewis (7)
Ysgol Gymraeg Bro Ogwr, Bridgend

The Tooth Fairy

The Tooth Fairy comes out at night
She won't come unless your eyes are shut tight
You put your tooth in your bed
And then you lie down your weary head
The Tooth Fairy leaves you money
Your mouth feels all kind of funny
You make a wish, you hope comes true
Nine times out of ten, they often do!

Bronwyn Siân Lewis (8)
Ysgol Gymraeg Bro Ogwr, Bridgend

James' Weird Day

James went to the beach
To find a peach
But all he could find was a leech
That he couldn't reach.

Then he went home
And saw a gnome
Sitting on a garden stone
Packing his bags to go to Rome!

As he went by
With a wink of his eye
He'd soon be flying high
So he shouted, 'Goodbye!'

As quick as that
Shot passed a cat
Chasing a rat
And that was that!

Natalia Saman (8)
Ysgol Gymraeg Bro Ogwr, Bridgend

Fireworks

F ireworks flying in the sky
I can see them flying high
R ockets shooting everywhere
E veryone just stops and stares
W e are having so much fun
O ver the rooftops like a gun
R ed, yellow, green and blue
K icking Catherine wheels are spinning too!

Chloe Harries (7)
Ysgol Gymraeg Bro Ogwr, Bridgend

Someone I Know

I know someone
Who can make a turtle face
Who watches 'Tracy Beaker'
And always wins the race!

She loves to get the hose out
On a hot summer's day
She even found a fossil
At the beach in Lulworth Bay!

She took part in the Christmas concert
She was the grumpy sheep!
She liked the roller coaster
She was too scared to peep!

I know this person the best
Because it's me!
I know myself
Better than anyone else you see!

Cari Haf Jones (7)
Ysgol Gymraeg Bro Ogwr, Bridgend

The Secret Room

I found a key
In an old oak tree
It was shining bright
In my sight.

It opened a door
And there was a roar
I ran away
And I may go back one day.

Ifan Lewis (7)
Ysgol Gymraeg Bro Ogwr, Bridgend

My Dragon

My dragon has a very long tail,
With scales as hard as chain mail.
His head is big and blue,
With a long nose and eyes, not one but two.
His feet only have three toes,
Where the other ones are, nobody knows.
My dragon likes to eat,
Lovely pigs and all fresh meat.
My dragon breathes fire
Like a burning tyre.
He flies up into the sky,
So high he doesn't have to try.
My dragon has wings like a big ship's sail
And best of all, he comes from Wales!

Cary Davies (7)
Ysgol Gymraeg Bro Ogwr, Bridgend

My Fairy

In the blink of an eye,
My little fairy flies on by,
Leaving a sparkly trail of dust,
She knows I'd love to see her,
I must, I must, I must!
What shall I call her,
So that she knows all is well,
To show her that she is the best?
It must be *Tinkerbell!*

Imogen Elyse Hunt (7)
Ysgol Gymraeg Bro Ogwr, Bridgend

My Kitten

I have a kitten
That's as soft as a mitten,
He's black and white
And sleeps all night.

He has lots of toys
That make lots of noise,
A round, bouncy ball
Which he hides in the hall.

He sometimes goes out,
But when I shout -
He comes running to see me
And purrs with great glee!

His name is Harry
He is so funny,
I wish that he'd stay
As small as a bunny!

Eleri Ann Lewis (7)
Ysgol Gymraeg Bro Ogwr, Bridgend

Honey

I love honey,
I think it's very funny,
Because it's very runny.
The sticky mess
Got on my dress,
My mum says I did not impress.
The bees make the honey,
When it's very sunny,
My daddy buys the honey,
He has lots of money,
So I can put it in my tummy,
Yummy!

Megan Lois Stephens (7)
Ysgol Gymraeg Bro Ogwr, Bridgend

Gobstoppers

I like chocolate, I like sweets,
I think gobstoppers are particularly neat.
I open my mouth so wide to put one in,
But it's so big, I have to pull down my chin.

I take a bite,
My teeth nearly break,
Sometimes,
I wish it was a cake.

I like red ones, green ones, purple and blue,
The best are big and round,
So big you can't fit two,
Without your chin touching the ground.

But if I had more than one,
I would share them with everyone,
If I had two or three
I would give one to Tesni,
But, and here is the twister,
To shut up my little sister!

Tomos Rhys Morgan (9)
Ysgol Gymraeg Bro Ogwr, Bridgend

Dolphins

D is for dolphins, diving down deep
O is for oceans, sparkling like light
L is for leaping, high into flight
P is for pod, playful and bright
H is for happy, helpful, having fun
I is for incredible, inquisitive friends
N is for noble, queens of the sea
   We all love dolphins, you and me!

Elen Lloyd (8)
Ysgol Gymraeg Bro Ogwr, Bridgend

Skateboarding

I love my board, it is so great,
I stay out until it is late, late, late!
The wheels go round and round,
When I ollie they hit the ground.
When it's teatime, in I come,
A couple of hours, my day is done,
Skating is so much fun, fun, fun!

Solomon Evans (8)
Ysgol Gymraeg Bro Ogwr, Bridgend

My Favourite Sports

I like rugby and football too
And run like a kangaroo
I jump and swim like a fish
But to be a footballer
That's my greatest wish!

Rhodri Lewis (8)
Ysgol Gymraeg Bro Ogwr, Bridgend

Bratz

Megan is brown,
Chloe is fair,
Jade has long, dark, wavy hair,
There are small ones too,
Fiona, Dana, Yasmin,
To name but a few
And boys too,
Bratz dolls, they're ace,
My favourite toys by far.

Hannah Steele (9)
Ysgol Gymraeg Bro Ogwr, Bridgend

My Hamster

Nasha is my hamster's name
We've trained her to be very tame
She is soft and cuddly and sleeps in her house
And through the day she's as quiet as a mouse.

She's awake at night
And as noisy as ever
She runs in her wheel
To show that she's clever.

She loves her food
Fruit and nuts she eats
She has to be good
To have a nice treat.

Sophie Davies (8)
Ysgol Gymraeg Bro Ogwr, Bridgend

My Family

My name is Jordan and I'm nearly nine
One the bus I go to school each day
And after tea, I go out to play
With my friends, Scott, Rhys and Ben
We play hide-and-seek after counting to ten
With Chelsea who's my big sister
We play a game and it's called Twister
Bruce, my dog, like to go to the park
He chases the ball and thinks it's a lark
My dad is a builder and he's very tall
He shows me how to build a wall
My mum, Maureen, she cooks, cleans and shops
She's the best - the very tops!

Jordan (8)
Ysgol Gymraeg Bro Ogwr, Bridgend

My Kitten

Cats sleep
    Anywhere
        Any table
            Any chair
                Top of piano
                    Window ledge
                        In the middle
                            On the edge
                                Open drawer
                            Empty shoe
                      Anybody's
                Lap will do
            Fitted in a
        Cardboard box
      In the cupboard
    With your frocks
Anywhere
    They don't care
        Cats sleep
            Anywhere
                My kitten is Stripes - *miaow!*

Hannah Jones (9)
Ysgol Gymraeg Bro Ogwr, Bridgend

Hallowe'en

H ere we are, in for a fright
A nother dark and windy, spooky night
L anterns aglow, we treat so slow
L ooking and listening for spooks in tow
O ut in the dark, shadows and noises about
W e try so hard not to scream and shout
E ach with a bag full of spooky treats to eat
E veryone ends up with smelly feet
N ow it's time to go to bed
    and dream about spooky things all around our heads.

Brittany Wilson (8)
Ysgol Gymraeg Bro Ogwr, Bridgend

I Wish I Was A Horse

I wish I was a horse
As bright as the sun
I wish I was a horse
As gold as a palomino
In my dreams I was a horse
That had strong wings
In my dreams I could see dust
From the stampede of different coloured horses
I woke up in a stable
With a horse lying right beside me
I shook my head to wake my brain
And *wow!*
My wishes had come true!

Llio Alaw Arfona Roberts (8)
Ysgol Gymraeg Bro Ogwr, Bridgend

Play As A Team

I am a rugby player
I play in a rugby team
We have to play together
Because teamwork has to be seen.

We ruck them
We tackle them
We pass to make a try
Together we are one
Tondu here we come!

'Who are, who are, who are we?
We are Tondu RFC
We can tackle
We can fight
We are made of dynamite!'

Nathan Watts (8)
Ysgol Gymraeg Bro Ogwr, Bridgend

The Zoo

When I was sitting at my desk,
One Friday afternoon,
Thoughts of the weekend,
Began to fill the room.

I thought about the zoo
And the animals, big and small,
Penguins, lions and the bears
And the giraffes, so big and tall.

I love to see the monkeys,
Swinging from tree to tree,
The camels walking, hump, hump, hump,
As they move around gracefully.

The pretty penguins, black and white,
Waddling like a clown,
They look so funny as they move,
Marching up and down.

Oh, I love the animals in the zoo,
They are lots of fun,
'Nia Roberts,' I hear Miss say,
Oh no, I must get my classwork done!

Nia Roberts (8)
Ysgol Gymraeg Bro Ogwr, Bridgend

When I Was . . .

When I was one year old,
It was so sad,
Because my teddy bear had been sold.
When I was four
I was taking a photo under the floor.
Now I'm ten
I can write with a pen.

Gruffydd Davies (8)
Ysgol Gymraeg Bro Ogwr, Bridgend

The Wardrobe

Step into the wardrobe
Maybe inside you'll see
Something extraordinary
Like a talking bear
Or dancing bee.

Step into the wardrobe
Maybe inside there'll be
Something really scrumptious
Like a chocolate flowing waterfall
Or a candyfloss tree.

Step into the wardrobe
Maybe inside will lead
To something quite exciting
Like a knight in shining armour
On his dappled steed.

Cian Griffiths (8)
Ysgol Gymraeg Bro Ogwr, Bridgend

Roald Dahl

What an amazing man!
From childhood to his dying day
From 'The Enormous Crocodile'
To 'Danny The Champion Of The World'
From pigs that can fly
To giants that are kind
That's why he wrote 'Revolting Rhymes'
Roald Dahl, Roald Dahl, Roald Dahl
His name is on every book
So why don't you buy and turn a page
In one of his special books!

Gwennan Jenkin (9)
Ysgol Gymraeg Bro Ogwr, Bridgend

Hallowe'en

Ghouls that drool,
Watch out for these monsters on the 31st of October
Trick or treat?
Get rewarded with sweets
What will you wear?
Vampires, witches, wizards
Or something else?
Watch out!

Keelan Birch (8)
Ysgol Gymraeg Bro Ogwr, Bridgend

My Family

My brother is a tearaway at home
He annoys me too much - he jumps on me and hits me.

When my mum has a cold, she has a red nose
Has she been drinking too much red wine?

My dad shouts like a lion
And sometimes it isn't my fault.

But I love them all so much
It is so good not be alone.

Rhys Huw Muzzupappa (8)
Ysgol Gymraeg Bro Ogwr, Bridgend

My Buffalo

My buffalo is very good
And sometimes bad
My buffalo is called Polo
Sometimes when he's really angry
He smashes down the trees
Oh, my buffalo is very good
But sometimes bad
And sometimes mad.

Richard John Hughes (9)
Ysgol Gymraeg Bro Ogwr, Bridgend

My Favourite Things

My favourite programme is 'Dr Who'
I like K-9 and the Daleks too
My favourite food is pizza and chips
And I do like ice cream
It's cold on my lips
My favourite place is the park
I always stay till it's nearly dark
And now my age has just gone seven
I can do what I like
I'm off to Devon!

Kairan Trebble (7)
Ysgol Gymraeg Bro Ogwr, Bridgend

When I Was . . .

When I was one I was very dumb
When I was two I tripped over my shoe
When I was three I was very naughty
When I was four I kicked the door
When I was five I learned to drive
When I was six I won the Grand Prix
When I was seven I went to Heaven
When I was eight I ate the gate
When I was nine I slept all the time.

Elliot Thomas (9)
Ysgol Gymraeg Bro Ogwr, Bridgend

My Bowling Trip

I went bowling yesterday
For my brother's birthday
With my mum and dad
And my friends
It came down to the last pin
Where I went on to win.

Lowri Urquhart (8)
Ysgol Gymraeg Bro Ogwr, Bridgend

My Hamster

My hamster is nasty
Like a lion
My hamster is playful
Like a puppy
He always hides
In his little house
He's always ready
To pounce
But he is mine
And I love him
PS, his name is Bobby.

John-Michael Wilkes (8)
Ysgol Gymraeg Bro Ogwr, Bridgend

The Man From Mars

I knew a man who came from Mars
He journeyed far among the stars
His hands were green
His legs were pink
And he tried to swim in the kitchen sink.

I did not intend
My little green friend
To die such a terrible way
But he's dead in a sack
That's shoved out the back
And the binmen are coming today.

Llewellyn Mercelsanca (8)
Ysgol Gymraeg Bro Ogwr, Bridgend

Some Of My Family

I have an older brother,
He is taller than my mum,
He teases me sometimes,
But we still have lots of fun.

I have a cousin who's a baby,
She's really funny too,
When I go to visit her,
She laughs and plays peekaboo.

My nana has a dog,
He is fluffy and small,
His name is Max
And he loves to play ball.

Curtis David (9)
Ysgol Gymraeg Bro Ogwr, Bridgend

The Happiness Of My Life

The happiness of my life is my dog, Molly
She is sweet, kind and jolly
She is long and tall
She sometimes falls
I love Molly even though she barks
At people, cats and dogs
And not just that
She puts a smile on my face too
So that makes her
The best dog in the world!

Cerys Siân Evans (8)
Ysgol Gymraeg Bro Ogwr, Bridgend